GOING PUBLIC

GOING PUBLIC

The Theory and Evidence on how
Companies Raise Equity Finance

TIM JENKINSON
ALEXANDER LJUNGQVIST

CLARENDON PRESS · OXFORD
1996

Oxford University Press, Walton Street, Oxford OX2 6DP

Oxford New York
Athens Auckland Bangkok Bogota Bombay
Buenos Aires Calcutta Cape Town Dar es Salaam
Delhi Florence Hong Kong Istanbul Karachi
Kuala Lumpur Madras Madrid Melbourne
Mexico City Nairobi Paris Singapore
Taipei Tokyo Toronto
and associated companies in
Berlin Ibadan

Oxford is a trade mark of Oxford University Press

Published in the United States
by Oxford University Press Inc., New York

British Library Cataloguing in Publication Data
Data available

Library of Congress Cataloging in Publication Data
Data available

ISBN 0-19-829077-2

10 9 8 7 6 5 4 3 2 1

Typeset by BookMan Services, Oxford
Printed in Great Britain
on acid-free paper by
Biddles Ltd., Guildford and King's Lynn

PREFACE

In recent years there has been an enormous amount of research interest in the way companies raise finance from stock markets. There are many reasons for this interest in 'initial public offerings' or IPOs, including:

- the fact that the capital-raising function of stock markets is particularly important in financing firms, many of which may be relatively small but fast growing;
- the growing competition between national stock exchanges for the custom of such small firms, with established markets such as NASDAQ trying to tempt non-US firms to list in the USA and Europe responding by launching two pan-European markets for small companies, EASDAQ and the Euro NM;
- two stylized facts appear to be valid in many countries, which a burgeoning theoretical literature has tried to explain: (i) IPOs are initially systematically underpriced, often by dramatic amounts, but (ii) they seem to underperform other companies over the longer term;
- the worldwide trend towards privatizing state-owned enterprises, which has raised many questions regarding the most appropriate way to sell companies to the public;
- a continuing policy debate regarding the most appropriate institutional arrangements to enable firms to access the stock market in an efficient manner, including the roles of financial intermediaries and institutional investors, and the rules laid down by stock exchanges.

Going Public is the first book to investigate these issues in a non-technical manner drawing upon international evidence from private-sector companies and privatizations. The book is intended as a specifically focused research monograph which, we hope, will be of considerable use to practitioners involved in IPOs, policy-makers interested in encouraging equity markets or in privatization issues, academics doing research in the area, non-specialist colleagues wishing to update their knowledge of the IPO literature for teaching or research reasons, and students of corporate finance.

T.J.J.
A.P.L.

Oxford,
June 1996

CONTENTS

PART III: POLICY IMPLICATIONS

Part I

THE IPO MARKET

1

INTRODUCTION

Whether or not to 'go public' is an important decision in the life cycle of a company. There are many attractions of having the shares in a company quoted on a stock exchange, including the ability to raise additional equity finance, the ability for the original entrepreneurs or investors to realize some of their investments, and the opportunity to set up employee share options plans. However, there are also costs. Not least among these are the financial costs of going public and the on-going costs of maintaining a quote on a stock exchange. There are also less quantifiable costs to the original owners in terms of corporate governance, ranging from the additional requirements to disclose information to, in some cases, the possibility of being subject to a hostile takeover bid.

Stock exchanges serve two main functions: to facilitate the raising of equity capital, and to enable trading in shares and other securities to take place. The capital-raising function is usually referred to as the primary market and the subsequent trading as the secondary market. It is important to an economy that both markets operate efficiently. If going public is relatively easy and inexpensive, this will increase the availability and lower the cost of equity finance. Similarly, a liquid and transparent secondary market will encourage investors to participate in the stock market and should again increase the availability of equity capital and lower investors' required returns. Even if new equity capital is not required, and the original investors simply want to sell part, or all, of their stake in a company, the ability to do this efficiently will encourage entrepreneurship and, ultimately, economic growth.

This book focuses on the efficiency of primary equity markets and, in particular, on the raising of new equity finance (for the benefit of either the company or the original owners) at the time of going public. This focus does not completely exclude further equity issues, such as rights issues in the UK or underwritten equity offers in the USA. However, although there is considerable international variation, in many countries the majority of companies raise external equity finance only once—by making an initial public offering (IPO) of their shares when they go public.[1] Thereafter, companies often rely upon retained earnings and debt (from banks or through issuing bonds) to finance their operations, and the importance of the stock exchange as a source of additional finance becomes less important. As a result, the efficiency of the IPO process, and the performance of companies that have gone public, has been the subject of considerable academic research. One of the aims of this book is to synthesize the enormous quantity of theoretical and applied research on IPOs, and to evaluate the contribution that academic research has made to our understanding of the costs and benefits of going public.

The important functions of an IPO in providing additional finance to companies and an 'exit route' for the original entrepreneurs and investors would be reason enough to justify considerable research interest. However, the scale of the academic research has been driven, in large part, by the existence of two apparent anomalies. First, there is now overwhelming international evidence of *initial underpricing*. That is, the shares in companies that go public are offered to investors at prices considerably below the price that they subsequently trade at on the stock market. Later in this chapter we describe the various IPO procedures and timing in more detail, but the important implication of initial underpricing is that it can be thought of as raising the cost—to the original owners—of raising equity finance. Second, there is a growing body of evidence that the shares of companies that go public suffer *long-run underperformance*. That is, relative to other quoted companies, investors appear to lose out by holding the shares of companies that have recently gone public. Such underperformance seems to last a surprising length of time, with some studies suggesting significant poor returns up to five years after the initial flotation.

Economists are intrigued and perplexed by such anomalies. They are intrigued first because the presence of such statistical anomalies may have implications for the underlying structure of financial markets. One important lesson that a company learns when it goes public

---

[1] It is possible to go public without undertaking an initial public offering, provided that the shares in the company are reasonably widely held. Going public without raising any new equity finance is often known as an *introduction* and is discussed in more detail below.

is that it cannot do it alone. Various financial intermediaries are involved in the IPO, including the investment bank that acts as a sponsor for the company, the underwriters of the share issue, and the brokers who find buyers for the shares. It is on the advice of these intermediaries that companies set the price of their shares. However, conflicts of interest sometimes arise. For example, if the sponsor also acts as the lead underwriter, then there may be some incentive to price the shares cheaply as underwriting risk is thereby reduced. Of course, if markets are competitive, one might expect that companies going public would be able to 'shop around' to find the financial intermediary who would offer the best price. However, in financial markets, where information is imperfect and reputations are all-important, the competitive paradigm of new entry being attracted in to correct such anomalies appears very strained.

An alternative way in which underpricing might, in principle, disappear is through potential purchasers bidding up the price of the shares. However, in some circumstances investors may not be able to participate in an issue, and so such competitive forces may be absent. Even when investors can participate in an IPO, it is not uncommon to observe considerable over-subscription for the shares, which necessitates the rationing of shares to investors. But it is not always the case that the offer price rises in the event of excess demand for the shares, as it would for example if the issue took place via a tender. We investigate many of these institutional and competitive issues in some detail in this book and draw implications for the design of efficient institutional structures.

The second important reason why economists have been intrigued by these apparent anomalies is that they both violate the fundamental tenet of 'no arbitrage'. In other words, the existence of systematic trading rules that make money should be transitory at best. The clear message from much of the work on long-run underperformance is that investors should sell the shares almost immediately they start trading (i.e. 'stag' the issue). In this way, investors fortunate enough to be allocated shares at the IPO would benefit from the initial underpricing but would not suffer the long-run underperformance. This is a simple trading rule that would be highly profitable, if the empirical observations were correct. Moreover, if people followed this rule, the dual phenomena would tend to disappear and no arbitrage profits would exist. Economists are perplexed when such trading rules persist, as they tend to indicate the irrationality of investors, or the uninformed nature of investors, or, perhaps, the size of transaction costs. We reassess the existing empirical evidence on these anomalies in Chapter 2.

Of course, if the empirical 'anomalies' are found to be particularly endemic and long lived, then a natural response is to reassess the reasons why they were viewed as anomalous in the first place. Much of the theoretical work on IPOs produced in recent years has considered whether it is possible to rationalize persistent initial underpricing as an equilibrium outcome of a consistent economic model. Various arguments have been advanced which suggest that companies might, under certain assumptions, *choose* to underprice their shares, ranging from the view that underpricing can act as a signal of the quality of the firm's management or future profitability to the belief that under-pricing is a form of insurance against possible legal action. Theoretical models that predict long-run underperformance are considerably less abundant, but various explanations have recently been advanced.

In the second part of the book we survey and critique the various theoretical explanations of IPO performance, drawing upon inter-national evidence to test their validity. Reference to data from many countries is particularly useful in this respect as the respective insti-tutional, regulatory, and legal differences often allow one to perform better tests of theoretical propositions. Although there are few countries in the world that have escaped an empirical study of IPO performance, much of the theoretical literature is still based on the US model of IPOs. But many of the predictions of this theoretical literature rely upon particular institutional and regulatory characteristics of the US stock market. The assumptions underlying some of the most widely advanced theories are often grossly violated in countries outside the USA. As a result, while many of the theories are certainly not inconsist-ent with US evidence, few of them can claim to explain the consistent international evidence on IPO underpricing and long-run under-performance. Part of the rationale of this book is to correct the US bias in the literature on IPOs and, in particular, to pay close attention to the various institutional arrangements and ways of going public that exist in different countries.

A final reason why IPOs have recently been the focus of much research is the worldwide trend towards privatization. Companies can be privatized in a variety of ways, such as through an outright sale to another company, or even via the distribution of free shares to members of the public. However, privatizations are often effected via an IPO, with the original shareholders (the government) selling shares to the public and, on occasions, raising additional finance for the company at the same time. Hence, privatizations are an important subset of total IPOs, although they are sometimes differentiated from private-sector flotations in that governments may have particular, frequently conflicting, objectives that they want to achieve through privatization (such as encouraging individual share ownership). We consider, in the third part of the book, evidence on how different privatization programmes have been executed and what constitutes best practice in privatization.

We also attempt to draw general policy conclusions for all IPOs based upon our survey of the theory and international evidence. There is a surprising degree of heterogeneity in the way companies go public in different countries, and it is possible to identify some 'models'—in the sense of rules, regulations and institutions—that work much better than others. For instance, a creative use of derivative securities—as seen in some privatization programmes—could help reduce the need to underprice a flotation.

In the remainder of this introductory chapter, we briefly discuss how companies are floated and the various costs—to the original owners—of going public.

1.1 How to Go Public

Companies can be floated in a variety of ways. The choice of technique for making an initial public offering tends to be influenced mainly by the size of the company, the uncertainty as to its value, and the institutional and regulatory arrangements in each particular country. Rather than attempt a comprehensive analysis of all the different ways of going public in each country, we focus on the five main methods that are widely observed: US-style firm commitment offers, UK-style offers for sale, private placements, book-building, and introductions.

1.1.1 Firm commitment offers

The most important method of taking a company public in the United States is via a firm commitment offering, and the majority of the theoretical work on IPOs takes this as its benchmark. Similar methods exist in many countries, although often the terminology differs, so we will describe the US firm commitment offering in some detail before discussing the variants that are observed elsewhere. Firm commitment offerings tend to be used by the majority of companies going public in the United States, especially in the case of medium to large sized offers.

In a firm commitment offering the lead manager will put together a syndicate of banks to underwrite the issue. The syndicate takes all of the shares on to its own books and is not allowed to pre-sell any of the issue to other investors. This *bought deal* technique of issuing clearly requires well capitalized issuing banks; the potential losses from a failed offer could be enormous.

The allocation of the stock is determined by the lead manager, and the distribution to individual syndicate members is not necessarily related to their underwriting positions. In the USA, there are no requirements that the shares should be distributed in a 'fair' way in the event of over-subscription. The lead manager will frequently discriminate between potential investors on the basis of judgements about whether they are likely to be relatively long-term investors. Investors who are suspected of being 'stags' (those who sell their allocations immediately) are often denied any shares, as their action would, *ceteris paribus*, tend to lower the share price once trading began. Institutional investors are also frequently rationed, as the lead manager would rather allocate a small core holding in the company to institutional investors in the expectation that they will buy additional shares in the after-market.

This description of the US firm commitment offering highlights some of the important distinguishing features of how firms go public. First, the way shares are distributed to investors varies considerably across countries. In the USA, distribution is typically achieved via brokers. This has the advantage that it is possible to establish good retail networks for new issues, rather than just relying upon the participation of institutional shareholders. It is straightforward for members of the public to participate in US IPOs, as information about forthcoming issues will be received via their brokers or specific IPO newsletters.

Second, the timing of the decision on the price of the shares and the quantity to be offered is an important consideration. In the USA, when a company files for registration with the Securities and Exchange Commission (SEC) in advance of making an IPO, it is merely required to set a likely range for the price of the shares. The actual price of the stock, and the quantity to be sold, is not fixed until the day of the issue, which enables the lead manager to establish what the demand curve for the stock looks like and also to take into account any short-term factors that may influence the likely success of the issue. Once the issue price has been set, the lead manager will distribute the shares, a process that is normally achieved in a few hours, and the shares will, in normal circumstances, begin trading immediately. Given these procedures, it is clear that the role of US underwriters is not really to bear substantial risk,[2] but rather to find a market for the shares and distribute them accordingly. In this latter role, the reputation of the issuing banks is likely to be very important.

Third, the allocation rules in the event of over-subscription vary across countries. In the USA, complete freedom is given to the lead manager to determine the final allocation of shares. This contrasts with many other countries (such as the UK, Singapore, Hong Kong, and Finland) where stock has to be rationed according to some 'fair' scheme, such as proportional scaling-down of allocations *pro rata*, or a lottery.

A final aspect of IPO arrangements that is worth noting is the use of techniques to support the price of the shares once they start trading in the after-market, often referred to as *price support*. In the USA price support is executed through the widespread use of *over-allotment options*. These work as follows. The company going public can grant to the lead investment bank the option to sell additional shares at the issue price. The purpose of this over-allotment option is to give the underwriting syndicate the ability to stabilize the price in the after-market without taking uncovered positions. These options can be for up to 15 per cent of additional shares. If there is a healthy demand for the shares, the investment bank can essentially go short, by selling additional shares, and can cover this position either by purchasing back shares in the after-market in the event of the share price falling below the issue price, or by exercising the option to sell more shares at the issue price if demand continues to be strong and the share price rises above the issue price.

The price support is terminated once the book is closed on the deal and the syndicate breaks up, which typically occurs within a week of

---

[2] One exception to this statement is when US underwriters have to play by other rules, as in the infamous case of the US portion of the 1987 British Petroleum privatization. As will be explained below, under the UK system the issue price is set some ten days before final distribution is achieved, which leaves the underwriters bearing considerable risk. The 1987 stock market crash occurred during this ten-day period, and resulted in massive losses for the US underwriting syndicate.

the listing. While such schemes introduce uncertainty into the final sum raised through an IPO, they allow a more accurate balance of supply and demand at the price that is fixed for the issue. It may also be possible to dampen short-run fluctuations in price that occur immediately the shares start trading without exposing the investment banks to excessive risk. Of course, it would be possible for the issuing bank to provide price support without the use of over-allotment options, simply by buying shares in the after-market if demand is weak, and taking them on to their own books. Until recently this type of un-covered price support was common in Germany,[3] although now price support is usually backed up by the granting of over-allotment options.

Many of these features of how a company goes public in the USA[4] are important in understanding the theoretical literature that has developed on IPOs—which has invariably taken the US system as its benchmark—and which we survey in Part II. However, there are relatively few countries in which IPOs occur via the equivalent of the firm commitment route; indeed, in many countries significantly different arrangements exist for taking companies public. We are interested in these differences not only because they allow us to test the applicability of the various theoretical explanations of the apparent IPO anomalies, but also from the policy perspective of designing efficient mechanisms for going public. To give a flavour of the international variation in how companies conduct IPOs, we focus on how arrangements differ in some of the other major markets, using the above classification of distribution, pricing, allocation, and trading.

1.1.2   Offers for sale

Methods of distributing the shares of companies going public differ

---

[3] In Germany price support can be provided for much longer than one week after the IPO.
[4] There is an alternative way of making an IPO in the USA, namely through a *best-efforts* contract with an investment bank. The special feature of a best-efforts agreement is that the issue is not underwritten. The investment bank agrees to distribute the shares, but if, after having made its best efforts, more than a certain proportion of the shares is left unsold, the whole issue can be withdrawn. The investment bank normally has 90 days to achieve the minimum sale. This set-up shifts the risk of the issue not succeeding on to the issuing firm. Best efforts contracts tend to be used for small companies: Ritter (1987) reports there were 364 best-efforts offers over the period 1977–82 raising an average of US$2.4 million. Over 70 per cent of all IPOs raising less than US$2 million were on a best-efforts basis, but virtually all offers over US$10 million used firm commitment offerings.

significantly between countries. Not all countries have an extensive network of brokers from whom members of the public buy shares. In some countries, notably Germany, banks perform the intermediary role, with all applications for IPOs being routed through the banks that make up the underwriting syndicate. However, in other countries, such as the UK, members of the public are often invited to apply for shares directly, through advertisements in newspapers. This method of issuing is known as an *offer for sale*. The company going public will usually sell all the shares to an issuing bank (the underwriter), which in turn arranges for the issue to be sub-underwritten, for a fee, by other financial institutions and large investors. In this way the issuing bank reduces the risks it faces if the issue is not a success. Members of the public then send requests for allocations directly to the issuing bank, which, once the offer period ends, decides how to allocate the shares. If there is insufficient demand for the shares, all requests are met in full and the underwriters take up any residual. If there is excess demand for the shares, the issuing bank is required to ration the shares according to some 'fair' scheme—which may take account of any subsidiary aims of the company, such as a wide shareholder base.

The advantages of this method of issuing are that the IPO is advertised very widely, all members of the public can subscribe very easily, and brokers' fees are avoided (although advertising costs can be high). We discuss estimates of the direct costs of making an IPO in more detail below. The main disadvantage of the offer for sale method is the relatively long period that is required between the fixing of the issue price and the close of the issue. For example, in the UK the price of the shares is fixed some ten days, on average, before trading begins. This is necessary because of the need to advertise the sale, distribute prospectuses, and allow individual investors time to complete the forms and return them to the issuing bank. As a result, underwriters can be exposed to considerable risk over this period. We return to this issue below when discussing pricing.

1.1.3 Private placements

Offers for sale tend to be used in the case of large issues in the UK, but most of the small to medium sized companies go public via a markedly different route, namely a *placing* (or, as it is known in other countries, a *private placement*). During a placing the issuing bank, effectively, underwrites the whole issue at an agreed price. The placing agreement is signed on *impact day*, which is usually around ten days before the shares start trading. However, the issuing bank will immediately arrange to place the shares with investors, although typically this task will be delegated to a specialist broker. In practice, the placing of the shares will normally be achieved on impact day, often within a couple of hours. The role of the issuing bank in this case is principally to arrange for the distribution of the shares rather than to bear risk.

An important distinction between placings and US firm commitment offerings is that in the former the shares are invariably bought by large institutional investors, who are often clients of the issuing bank or broker. The general public is, in practice, virtually excluded from the initial offering, although they are, of course, able to buy shares in the after-market. Placings are usually cheaper than offers for sale for smaller companies.

1.1.4 Book-building

A fourth method of distributing shares that is becoming popular in some European countries, and which has many of the features of firm commitment offering, is book-building. For example, in Germany in 1995 all but one IPO took the form of a book-building. There are three stages to a book-building exercise. First, there is the pre-marketing stage during which the issuing bank determines demand by eliciting non-binding bids for the shares. Based upon this information, a minimum and maximum price is set. The second stage is the book-building proper, when investors (both retail and institutional) bid within the price range, stating a price and quantity combination. The issuing bank uses these bids to set the final offer price. All investors pay the same offer price, even if they bid higher. The issuing bank has complete discretion over the allocation of shares; there is no requirement to be 'fair'. In the third and final stage trading begins; the issuing bank will often support prices by buying in the after-market, and is typically granted an over-allotment option to cover its position.

The main difference between book-building and firm commitment offerings is the use of a formal tender in the second stage, as opposed to the informal tender that occurs in the latter. However, the issuing bank, in consultation with the company, still sets the price of the shares rather than allowing the tender process itself to equate supply and demand. In practice, the issuing banks have tended to price the IPOs to generate modest jumps in price on the first trading day.

An obvious alternative to the methods of distribution and pricing discussed above would be to conduct a formal tender, especially given the uncertain market valuation of many companies going public. Until quite recently, offers for sale by *tender* were common in the UK. For example, in 1983, 15 of the 24 offers for sale in that year were on a tender basis. However, no private sector IPOs by tender have taken place in the UK since 1986, although part of the British Airports Authority (BAA) privatization in 1987 was conducted via a tender. Indeed, this latter issue had an interesting feature in that investors paid what they bid for the shares, rather than the more normal procedure of a single strike price being set once all bids have been received. The reasons for the demise of tenders in the UK are unclear; certainly no regulatory impediments have been introduced. Fashion has tended to favour hybrid issues with part of the issue being sold via an offer for sale and part by placing.

While tenders have fallen out of favour in the UK, in Japan regulatory changes in the wake of the Recruit Cosmos scandal (see Chapter 2) have made tenders compulsory when companies are floated. The Japanese system is interesting in that a formal tender is used for a portion of the issue, and the price determined by the tender is then used to fix the price of the remaining shares. Within the tender investors pay the price they bid, as in the BAA example above, with shares being allotted to the highest bidders until the tender issue becomes fully allocated. The price used to sell the remainder of the shares is then set at the weighted average of the successful bid prices from the tender. Kaneko and Pettway (1994) document how initial underpricing has fallen significantly since these regulatory changes were introduced, from around 70 per cent in the mid-1980s to 12 per cent in the early 1990s.

1.1.5 Introductions

A final route via which companies can go public in some countries, which by definition avoids problems of initial underpricing, is via an introduction. No shares are sold during an introduction: the shares are simply introduced to the market and trading in them commences. However, companies have to satisfy the listing requirements of the relevant stock exchanges, which normally impose limits on the minimum number of shareholders (to promote liquidity in the after-market) and a minimum proportion of the equity capital in the hands of the 'public'.

A possible advantage of an introduction is that the original share-holders benefit from the ability to trade their shares on a stock exchange, but do not suffer the 'cost' of the initial underpricing that occurs if they sell a proportion of their holding via an IPO. If they want to realize some, or all, of their investment, they can do this at a later date by selling at the price established by the market.

There are many more details of how IPO procedures differ around the world, but most are either hybrids or restricted versions of the models outlined above. Thumbnail sketches of the main features of IPOs in 25 different countries are provided in Loughran, Ritter, and Rydqvist (1994), although regulations and procedures change regularly.

Before moving on to the stylized facts on initial underpricing and long-run underperformance, we briefly discuss the direct and indirect costs of going public.

1.2 The Costs of Going Public

Economists argue that going public involves two types of cost. First, there are the *direct costs* of an issue, for example underwriting fees, legal expenses, accountancy, and audit fees in addition to the less quantifiable costs in terms of management time. Many of these costs are relatively fixed, and so there are considerable economies of scale. For example, Jenkinson (1990) estimated the average direct costs of issues raising less than US$8 million in the UK at 10.4 per cent of the gross proceeds, falling to 5.2 per cent for issues raising more than US$16 million. Similar trends are reported for the USA, where direct costs account for around 18.2 per cent on average of small issues raising less than US$5 million, falling to 6.8 per cent for issues raising over US$100 million.

The second category of cost comprises the *indirect costs* associated with the initial underpricing. It is usually argued that initial under-pricing constitutes a transfer of wealth from the original owners of the company to the new shareholders, and as such should be regarded as a cost of raising equity finance.

Of course, there are plausible reasons to expect some limited under-pricing of IPOs on average. First, transaction costs are not negligible on any equity market, with bid–ask spreads often being a few percentage points, depending on the liquidity of the stock. If an investor is to be enticed to change her portfolio, she may require a limited incentive in the form of an initial discount. Second, there is a risk that the market price may fall below the issue price. If IPOs were priced, on average, with zero discount, risk averse investors would, in the absence of specific information that would allow them to discriminate between winners and losers, prefer to buy shares in the after-market. Hence, the initial discount on IPOs might be interpreted as a return for bearing risk. However, as will be seen in the next chapter, observed initial underpricing is typically too large to be explained away in this way.

Two types of shares can be sold at an IPO: primary equity, and secondary equity. The former are new shares sold to investors, the proceeds from which will accrue to the company; the latter are shares owned by the original investors in the company, some of which may be sold at the IPO, with the proceeds accruing to the original investors. In practice, some IPOs consist of all primary equity, with the original investors retaining their shares, some IPOs are all secondary equity, with no new money being raised for the company, but with the original owners selling some of their shares, and many consist of a combination of the two.

In the case of sales of secondary equity, the wealth loss associated with underpricing is obvious: the original shareholders could have sold their shares at a higher price had they retained them and sold them in the after-market. In the case of primary equity sales, the wealth loss occurs via the *dilution* of the original shareholders' stakes in the company. Initial underpricing of the IPO will mean that the new investors acquired their stake in the company for less than it was worth, to the detriment of the original shareholders. Put another way, in the absence of underpricing, the company could have raised the same sum of money by selling fewer shares, and thereby would have avoided diluting the holdings of the original investors.

From this discussion, it is clear that the extent of the wealth loss arising from initial underpricing will depend crucially upon the proportion of shares (old and new) sold at the IPO. If no shares are sold, as in the case of an introduction, then no wealth loss occurs. At the other extreme, if the original investors sell all their secondary shares at the IPO, any underpricing loss will apply to their entire holding. Of course, between these two extremes, the original investors may be tempted to view an initial jump in the share price as being beneficial to them: their retained holding is now worth more than expected. But this does not remove the fact that any shares they sold at the IPO could have been sold for more.

In summary, the performance of IPOs are of considerable interest to all parties involved in equity markets:

- to *investors*, because they can hope to gain above-average returns by buying shares at subscription and selling them almost immediately, to avoid long-run underperformance;
- to *issuers*, since underpricing means lower flotation proceeds, which—when adding in the substantial direct costs of coming to market—may tip the balance against going public, while poor long-run performance may raise the cost of capital in subsequent equity (or debt) financing exercises;
- to the firms' *old owners*, because they suffer the cost of underpricing on the shares they sell at flotation, and the opportunity cost of abnormally poor performance on the shares they retain;
- to *underwriters*, whose role as intermediaries leaves them open to the twin challenge of simultaneously pricing too high (from the point of view of subscribers who suffer long-run losses) and too low (from the point of view of the issuing firms which forgo funds when their offerings are underpriced), and who are themselves adversely affected by long-run underperformance as potential issuers will not be keen to come to market (the supply side) nor will investors wish to subscribe (the demand side) if IPOs systematically and consistently underperform alternative investments;
- to *policy-makers*, not because the systematic patterns in pricing and performance would call for intervention—other than removing restrictions on short sales to help the market arbitrage away any systematic mispricing—but because they may want to facilitate stock market listings (say, by removing tax disadvantages) to provide small and medium-sized firms with cheap and efficient access to investment finance;
- and finally to *academics*, since the persistent and systematic nature of anomalous returns raises challenging questions about the informational efficiency of capital markets.

In the next chapter we consider the international evidence on initial underpricing and long-run underperformance before turning, in Part II, to the theoretical explanations that have been proposed. Part III will discuss the lessons from two decades of privatization in the UK and elsewhere, and will attempt to draw policy conclusions on what constitutes best practice in taking companies public, be they private-sector or public-sector enterprises.

2

STYLIZED FACTS

2.1 Introduction

2.1.1 The new issue market

While the USA and the UK have had vibrant primary equity markets for a long time, IPOs have made a significant appearance in much of continental Europe and the liberalizing economies in Latin America and Asia only since the 1980s. In some countries, private-sector firms have gone public in the wake of large-scale government privatization programmes, as in Chile and Mexico, while in others, tax changes, deregulation of investment restrictions on institutional and foreign investors, and generational change have prompted entrepreneurs to seek fresh funds from the stock exchange or to liquidate share holdings by selling to a dispersed group of investors.

One way to illustrate the recent popularity of initial public offerings is to compare the numbers of listed domestic companies in 1994 and in 1981. Since the change in this number is net of delistings, such a comparison will tend to understate the occurrence of flotations. The diagrams in Figure 2.1 graph the percentage increase in listings for 18 industrialized and 36 emerging stock markets. With very few exceptions—mainly in the developed world—there are many more listed firms now than there were at the start of the 1980s. Even in those industrialized economies where there was a fall in listings, a large number of firms did go public—but these were swamped by an even larger number of delistings arising from mergers, hostile takeovers, leveraged buy-outs, or financial distress.

The number of quoted firms increased the most in emerging markets. It rose 26-fold in Indonesia, and more than doubled in 13 other countries. To illustrate, a mere 23 firms were listed on the Lisbon Stock Exchange in 1981, compared with 195 in 1994. In the industrialized

Fig. 2.1. Increase in the number of listed domestic companies, 1981–1994

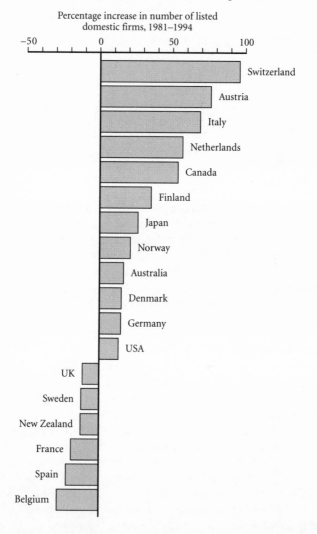

(*a*) **Developed markets**

Source: Emerging Stock Markets Fact-Book (International Finance Corporation, Washington), except for Germany (Bundesbank) and the UK (Stock Exchange Quarterly). Base year differs from 1981 in Finland (1983) and New Zealand (1984).

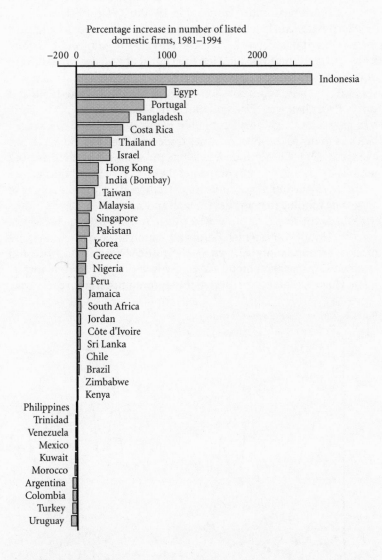

(*b*) **Emerging markets**

Source: Emerging Stock Markets Fact-Book (International Finance Corporation, Washington).
Base year differs from 1981 in Colombia (1982), Kuwait (1985), Sri Lanka (1985), Turkey
(1982), and Venezuela (1982).

world, the largest increase occurred in Switzerland, where the total number of listings jumped from 121 in 1981 to 237 in 1994.

Data on the actual number of flotations are available for a handful of the above markets. Figure 2.2 illustrates the 1980s 'going public boom' in seven representative countries: the United States, the United Kingdom, Germany, Korea, Sweden, Hong Kong and Finland. In some of these, many more companies were taken public during the 1980s and early 1990s than were listed in 1981. Finland provides a particularly striking example: 95 firms went public between 1981 and 1994, almost twice as many as the 49 companies traded on the Helsinki Stock Exchange in 1981. Clearly, therefore, going public has enjoyed increasing popularity among private companies the world over, and thus merits attention as a favoured exit route for entrepreneurs and a key source of corporate funding to many firms, small and large.

Outside the Anglo-Saxon world, this may come as something of a surprise. Many continental European countries and the emerging markets are commonly believed to rely more heavily on bank loans and retained earnings than on public equity in funding corporate investment. However, while it is true that these economies still have relatively

Fig. 2.2. IPO volume in selected countries

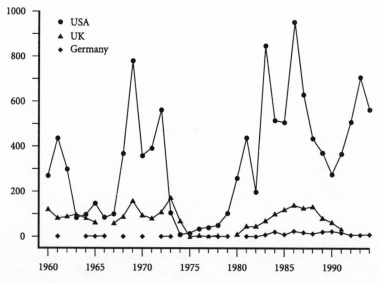

(*a*) The USA, UK, and Germany

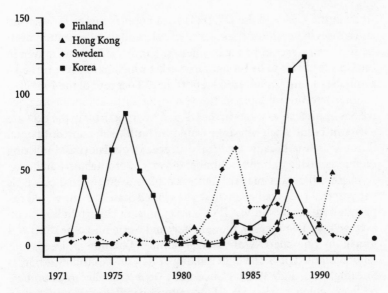

(*b*) Korea, Sweden, Hong Kong, and Finland

Acknowledgements: We are grateful to the following for sharing their IPO data with us: Matti Keloharju (Finland), Paul McGuinness (Hong Kong), Kristian Rydqvist (Sweden), and Jay Ritter (USA). Data for the other countries are from: Loughran, Ritter, and Rydqvist (1994) and Vaughan, Grinyer, and Birley (1977) (UK), the Korean Stock Exchange's annual *Fact Book* (Korea), and Ljungqvist's database (Germany). UK data were unavailable for 1966, 1979, and 1992–4. The end dates for the Korean, Swedish, Hong Kong, and Finnish series are 1990, 1993, 1991, and 1994 respectively.

small equity markets compared with the Anglo-Saxon countries, their recent appetite for initial public offerings does point to an interesting reversal in traditional patterns of corporate finance.

2.1.2 International differences in the use of initial public offerings

It would be wrong, however, to conclude that the rest of the world has at last converted to the Anglo-Saxon love affair with the stock market, for Europe's IPOs are quite a different breed from their US and UK cousins. First, they involve mostly old, large, well-established companies rather than start-up ventures in risky new industries. The median age among continental European offerings is 50 years, which contrasts with the typical US IPO firm, which is 6 years old when taken public. Second, machine tool manufacturers, banks, and other such traditional industries dominate most continental European new issue markets, while in the USA and the UK IPOs are a popular means for start-up enterprises in new industries to attract risk capital or for venture capitalists to exit stakes in young businesses. Third, it is not uncommon in the USA for firms to be brought to market which have never turned a profit: Beatty and Zajac (1995) report that 58 per cent of the 1984 IPO cohort were unprofitable in the year prior to flotation. Recent flotations by biotech ventures in the UK and Internet firms in the USA are a case in point. Such offerings would be unthinkable in continental Europe, not least because the firms concerned would not pass the listing requirement of a minimum number of years of profitable trading.

These differences matter. Figure 2.3 plots average gross proceeds per year in 11 selected countries. The United States, as one would expect, has by far the busiest IPO market, raising US$6.6 billion in an average year. Remarkably, though, Italy and Germany come third and fourth in our chart, with average annual flotation proceeds not far behind the UK's! The high ranking of Italy and Germany is not, as one might conclude at first glance, due to exceptionally large numbers of firms going public: UK IPOs outnumbered Italian or German ones by a factor of six or more in the 1980s. Rather, the ranking is due to companies in the two continental countries tapping the market for much larger amounts of cash: the median flotation raised US$77 million and US$37 million in Italy and Germany, respectively, compared with US$11 million and US$10.5 million for the median American and British IPO.

In parts of continental Europe, a much larger fraction of this cash goes into the original owners' pockets rather than being invested in the firm: 67 and 23 per cent of Portugal's and Germany's flotations, respectively, involve *only* shares sold by insiders, rather than primary shares originating in a capital increase. By contrast, 98 per cent of American IPOs involve at least some primary equity, and 56 per cent sell solely new shares. The average split between primary and secondary equity is 85:15 in the USA, but as low as 58:42 in Sweden (Högholm and Rydqvist, forthcoming) or Germany (Ljungqvist 1995a), or 54:46 in the UK (Brennan and Franks 1995). Other European countries are less driven by the insiders' desire to realize their investments: the fraction of firms selling only primary shares is even higher, at 73 per cent, in Finland than in the USA. Outside Europe, indications are that the pattern is similar to the American one: only 3 per cent of Korean flotations are exclusively secondary.

In summary, there are two distinct trends in the way initial public

Fig. 2.3. Average annual and median gross proceeds in selected countries

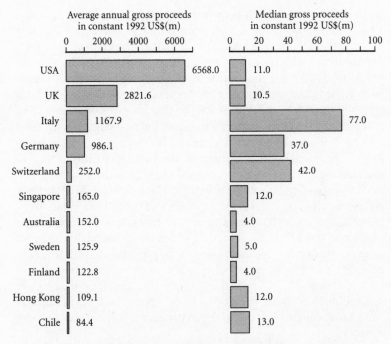

Sources: USA—own calculations based on Ibbotson *et al.* (1994); UK—Jenkinson (1990), excluding privatizations; other countries—own calculations based on Loughran *et al.'s* (1994) Tables 1 and 2. In the left-hand graph, average annual gross proceeds for each country are calculated as: mean gross proceeds times number of firms, divided by number of years covered by the study. Median gross proceeds is for firm commitment offerings only in the USA and for placings only in the UK. Sources that do not use populations have as far as possible been excluded, to avoid biases in computation.

offerings are used internationally. First, in some countries it is predominantly older and larger firms that are taken public by their owners in an attempt to realize capital gains. In others, a flotation is intended primarily to raise further funding for what are usually small and young growth companies. The implications for pricing and valuation are very different in the two cases, for two reasons: (i) offerings by mature firms should be easier to price than those by untried and unknown companies; and (ii) the more the original owners participate in the IPO by selling their own shares, the more of a personal interest they have in getting the offer price right.

2.1.3 Stylized facts

While much of the early literature on initial public offerings has been written in response to the US experience, there is now a growing body of international research which has confirmed the main stylized facts previously found in the American new issue market. As outlined in the previous chapter, the most extensively documented empirical regularity is the initial underpricing phenomenon: first-day trading prices typically exceed the price at which the shares were sold to investors. A second stylized fact—which we discuss below—concerns the time series behaviour of first-day returns and IPO volume: there are cycles in both the extent of underpricing and the number of firms coming to market. Lastly, a more recent empirical anomaly is the poor long-run performance of initial public offerings. The following three sections will present the empirical evidence on each of these. The availability of international research presents an opportunity to assess the robustness of the proposed theoretical models which try to rationalize the new issue phenomena. As we mentioned in the previous chapter, these explanations are almost exclusively predicated on an analysis of the US IPO market and thus may fail to explain why, despite differences in institutional and other conditions across countries, IPOs are underpriced and seem to perform poorly in the after-market in almost every country.

2.2 Underpricing

2.2.1 The international evidence

Probably the earliest empirical regularity in the new issue market to have attracted attention is the fact that companies apparently underprice their shares when going public. This implies on the one hand a handsome profit for those investors lucky enough to obtain stock in the offering, and on the other an opportunity cost of going public to the company's old owners. Initial underpricing may be one reason why—the IPO wave of the 1980s notwithstanding—so far relatively few eligible firms have chosen to go public in many major economies, Germany being an obvious example.

Table 2.1 lists comparative evidence of IPO underpricing in a large number of countries. Most evidence comes from the USA, while studies on other countries are more recent, reflecting the increased frequency

of flotations in the 1980s and 1990s. The first-day premium that subscribers experience is positive in virtually every country, and typically
averages more than 15 per cent in industrialized countries and close to
60 per cent in emerging markets, measured between subscription and
the first day of trading. These averages hide some cases of enormous
underpricing; in Malaysia, for instance, the average new issue between
1978 and 1983 started trading at a 167 per cent premium over its offer
price.

There are several reasons why emerging-market IPOs are so much
more underpriced than US or European ones. Political and bureaucratic meddling is one of them. While countries such as Taiwan and
Korea have recently liberalized the way in which issuers and underwriters can determine the flotation price, the evidence summarized in
the table mostly pre-dates such regulatory reform and hence reflects
the effect of administrative fiat. For instance, prior to the 1988 partial
deregulation, Korean firms had to price their shares at book value,
while until 1993 Taiwanese offering prices were calculated using a
formula based on the price–earnings ratio and other characteristics of
three supposedly 'comparable' firms.

Favouritism is another form of political interference that has been
rife in many countries, both emerging and developed. In Malaysia, new
issues have been used not only to aid ethnic policy, but also—or so it
has been alleged—to line the pockets of the politically influential:
while the law requires ethnic Malays (as opposed to ethnic Chinese) to
be allocated a minimum of 30 per cent of shares in equity offerings,
generous allocations of deeply discounted stock have allegedly found
their way into the hands of a privileged few, in spite of an otherwise
ostensibly fair *pro rata* allocation system modelled on the UK example.
More notoriously, the Japanese Recruit Cosmos scandal has become a
byword for corruption: in April 1989 Japan's prime minister was forced
to resign when in was revealed that the Recruit Company had attempted to buy political influence via targeted allocations of highly
underpriced shares in its spun-off Cosmos subsidiary. Thus, in some
countries offer prices are set on the basis not only of who you are, but
also of who you want to please. In the wake of Recruit Cosmos, Japan
relaxed regulations concerning the pricing of IPOs while tightening
allocation rules. The move to letting offering prices be determined by
auction has substantially reduced average underpricing, from about 70
per cent to 12 per cent. Similar effects of deregulation are evident in
Korea and other liberalizing countries.

Table 2.1. Comparative evidence of IPO underpricing

Country[a]	Study	Sample period	Sample size	Initial return (%)[b]
USA	Ibbotson *et al.* (1994)	1960–92	10,626	15.3
USA	Ritter (1987)[c]	1977–82	664	14.8
USA	Ritter (1987)[d]	1977–82	364	47.8
Australia	Finn and Higham (1988)	1966–78	93	29.2
Australia	Lee *et al.* (1994)	1976–89	266	11.9
Belgium	Manigart and Rogiers (1992)	1984–90	28	13.7
Canada	Jog and Srivastava (1996)	1971–92	254	7.4
Finland	Keloharju (1993a)	1984–92	91	14.4
France	Jacquillat (1986)[e]	1972–86	87	4.8
Germany	Ljungqvist (1996b)	1970–93	180	9.2
Great Britain	Jenkinson and Mayer (1988)[f]	1983–86	143	10.7
Great Britain	Jenkinson and Mayer (1988)[g]	1983–86	68	4.7
Great Britain	Jenkinson and Mayer (1988)[h]	1983–86	26	−2.2
Italy	Cherubini and Ratti (1992)	1985–91	75	29.7
Japan	Jenkinson (1990)	1986–88	48	54.7
Japan	Kaneko and Pettway (1994)[i]	1989–93	37	12.0
Netherlands	Buijs and Eijgenhuijsen (1993)	1982–91	72	7.4
New Zealand	Vos and Cheung (1992)	1979–91	149	28.8
Spain	Fernandez *et al.* (1992)	1985–90	71	35.4
Sweden	Rydqvist (1993)	1970–91	213	39.0
Switzerland	Kunz and Aggarwal (1994)	1983–89	42	35.8
Brazil	Aggarwal *et al.* (1993)	1979–90	62	78.5
Chile	Aggarwal *et al.* (1993)	1982–90	19	16.3
Hong Kong	McGuinness (1992)	1980–90	80	17.6
Korea	Dhatt *et al.* (1993)	1980–90	347	78.1
Malaysia	Dawson (1987)	1978–83	21	166.6
Mexico	Aggarwal *et al.* (1993)	1987–90	37	33.0
Portugal	Alphao (1989)	1986–87	62	54.4
Singapore	Koh and Walter (1989)	1973–87	66	27.0
Taiwan	H. L. Chen (1992)	1971–90	168	45.0
Thailand	Wethyavivorn and Koo-Smith (1991)	1988–89	32	58.1

[a] The table presents results for three groups of countries: the USA, other developed countries, and emerging markets. The classification into developed and emerging markets follows the financial indicators section in *The Economist*.

[b] Initial returns may be measured between the (first) subscription day and the first trading day, or some day soon after trading starts. They may be gross or net of the concurrent market return. Generally, results are robust to market-return adjustments and the choice of time

Table 2.1.   (*cont.*)

frame. Averages are calculated using equal weights. Apart from in the USA, capitalization-weighted or gross-proceeds-weighted averages would not be significantly different.
   [c] Firm commitment offerings only.
   [d] Best-efforts offerings only.
   [e] Tender offers only.
   [f] Placings.
   [g] Fixed-price offers.
   [h] Tender offers.
   [i] Auctions, compulsory since 1989.

As in Japan after 1989, auction-like offering mechanisms such as tenders in the United Kingdom, the Netherlands and Belgium, or *offres publiques de vente* in France, are generally associated with low levels of underpricing; most Chilean IPOs have also used auctions, and have been modestly underpriced, at least by emerging-market standards. This is not particularly surprising, given that, unlike fixed-price offers, tenders allow market demand to at least partly influence the issue price. What is curious, though, is that we do not observe a shift towards greater use of auctions: tenders are rare in most European countries (Finland, Germany, Italy, Sweden, Switzerland) despite the absence of regulatory restrictions on the way firms price their shares. Moreover, they have become increasingly uncommon in the Netherlands and have disappeared altogether in the United Kingdom, which indicates that the minimization of underpricing is not the prime concern in a firm's choice of selling procedure. In the United States, underpricing also varies systematically with the choice of offering mechanism: *ex post* discounts are markedly lower in firm-commitment than in best-efforts offerings. Given the discussion in Chapter 1, this is not surprising: exceptionally risky firms would find it both difficult and expensive to obtain underwriting cover and hence typically turn to best-efforts contracts instead.

2.2.2 Discussion

Economists studying the underpricing phenomenon long used to term it a puzzling anomaly. In an efficient and perfect market, theory suggests, companies should not 'leave money on the table', certainly not in such large quantities. While the evidence from some emerging markets and from pre-Recruit Japan could easily be dismissed as the none-too-surprising outcome of corruption or bureaucratic pricing mechanisms almost deliberately designed to obstruct market forces, the same cannot presumably be said of the US or European experience.

In trying to explain why firms are floated at too low a price, economists have generated a large theoretical and empirical literature, whose main line of attack is the assumption of market perfection and efficiency. Depending on the approach, underpricing becomes an efficient form of compensation for investors, induces underwriters to exert optimal selling effort, or serves as insurance against future potential litigation by disaffected shareholders. Part 2 of this book will review these contributions in some detail. Almost invariably, underpricing is seen as involuntary but unfortunately necessary, even in the signalling approach, which assumes that high-quality firms use underpricing as a signal to lower their cost of capital in subsequent funding exercises: if there were a cheaper way to signal quality, presumably firms would choose not to underprice their offerings.

However, few theories can account for the fact that practitioners view a discounted flotation as a *success* which will tend to get the firm a good press. When Sock Shop International went public on the London Stock Exchange in 1987, its chief executive pronounced herself 'ecstatic' at the flotation being underpriced by 65 per cent.[1] To an economist this is extraordinary: selling an asset at well below its market value is not usually cause for celebration. This raises two questions: who stands to lose from underpricing, and are there benefits to discounting one's IPO?

The main cost is borne by the previous owners. This is obviously true if some of the shares offered to the public come out of their stakes, in which case the owners fail to realize the full value of their investments. But even if they do not participate in the offering—that is, if all shares on offer are primary—the old owners have to dilute their stakes more the more highly underpriced the IPO: for a given funding need, the lower the offer price, the greater the number of shares that need to be sold. It is worth noting, however, that the traditional measures of underpricing reported in Table 2.1 greatly overstate the original shareholders' wealth losses. Only a shareholder who sold her entire stake would experience the headline underpricing loss, whereas if she retained at least some shares the opportunity of selling in the aftermarket would remain. In Germany, for instance, IPOs are underpriced by 10 per cent on average, but the old owners lose a much lower 4 per cent of their pre-flotation wealth. Owner-related losses are lower than subscriber-related underpricing would suggest, partly because a great number of new issues involve no insider sales, and partly because retention rates when insiders do participate in the offering tend to be high, in Germany and elsewhere.

Counteracting these costs are a number of potential benefits. Underpriced offers are typically heavily oversubscribed. Whether the publicity generated by having to ration subscribers, or even turn them away, outweighs the underpricing cost is an open question, but many practitioners seem to interpret the extent of excess demand as an indicator of a flotation's success. Another, more readily acceptable, benefit is the insurance against under-subscription that underpricing provides. It could be argued that the disutility associated with one's offering being left with the underwriters greatly exceeds the reduction in utility arising from greater dilution or lower realized gains. The 4 per cent figure for Germany would suggest that such an insurance policy is not all that expensive for the original owners.

Lastly, while underpricing may lead to the financial dilution of the insiders' retained stakes, it may also, perversely perhaps, ensure that their control is *not* diluted. The point is that excess demand affords the issuer the opportunity to choose a shareholder base of its liking. Since underpriced flotations almost invariably have to be rationed, the greater is underpricing, the smaller is the average *pro rata* allocation and thus the less is the likelihood of future challenges to the old owners' control.

On balance, therefore, underpricing need not only be a cost of going public, variously rationalized in the early literature on the subject as an involuntary but necessary compensation, signalling or insurance device: it may also have desirable side-effects which outweigh the costs of forgone capital gains and dilution.

2.3 Cycles in IPO Volume and Initial Returns

2.3.1 When do firms go public?

The conceived wisdom in finance textbooks is that issuing corporate securities in an efficient market should not be a positive net present value (NPV) transaction, meaning that the timing of a financing decision should not matter since any offering will be fairly priced.[2] It

---

[2] See, for instance, Brealey and Myers (1991), p. 289.

might be tempting, therefore, to conclude that IPOs occur randomly over time. However, this is not what we observe in practice. As Figure 2.2 above showed, the number of firms coming to market is far from random, but rather shows signs of positive auto-correlation: periods of high IPO volume are likely to be followed by further heavy IPO activity.[3] Even where there is no apparent auto-correlation, IPO volume is heavily clustered, as in Finland, where the great majority of new issues occurred in only two years, 1987 and 1988. Moreover, as we remarked earlier, outside the Anglo-Saxon countries, going public has mainly been a phenomenon of the 1980s and 1990s.

How can we square these patterns with the textbook paradigm? Unlike a bond issue, say, or some other form of financing decision, going public is a much less reversible step which has implications far beyond simply raising funds. Even if we accept the tenet that the sale of shares to investors is a zero-NPV transaction, such that firms cannot take advantage of the market by selling overpriced shares, the decision to go public in the first place presumably needs to be a positive-NPV proposition. Hence, the stream of companies coming to market should depend on factors that determine the trade-off between the costs and benefits of a stock market listing. When these factors vary over time, so will the number of firms seeking a quotation.

Listing and other requirements imposed by the stock exchange can affect the costs of going public both directly and indirectly. For instance, a reduction in listing fees or publicity and compliance requirements would make a flotation more attractive financially.[4] A relaxation of listing rules could also increase the non-financial attraction of going public. A reduction in the minimum float requirement or an easing of restrictions on the issuance of lower- or non-voting stock would decrease the likelihood of future loss of control and hence the costs of subjecting one's firm to the (presumably) greater scrutiny of a public equity market. Similarly, the less information needs to be disclosed, both in the IPO prospectus and on an on-going basis, the better the company can protect its strategic position relative to its competitors.

A major cost in the IPO process is the commission paid to inter-

---

[3] In the USA, for instance, Ibbotson and Jaffe (1975) report auto-correlation in the region of 75 per cent in monthly IPO volume during the 1960s.

[4] Disclosure requirements in the USA have gradually been reduced since the enactment of the 1933 Securities Act. A typical registration statement nowadays rarely runs to more than 50 pages. By (extreme) contrast, when Republic Steel went public in 1934, it filed a 19,897 page registration document with the SEC! (Van Arsdell 1958)

mediaries, such as financial advisors and underwriters. The more competitive the market for these services, the lower in general the cost. Entry into the industry would increase competitiveness but in some countries is restricted by law. In this vein, one may speculate that repealing the Glass–Steagall Act, which bars commercial banks from underwriting equity offerings, would lower direct IPO costs in the USA. It might also lead to less underpricing, if banks chose to compete not only on underwriting spreads but also on the offer price they promise potential issuers. If the original owners care about dilution of control, they will tend to take their firms public in periods of high stock market valuations, since for a given funding need a higher offer price implies less dilution. Thus, IPO volume should be related to the stock market climate. It should also vary with the availability of investment opportunities and hence the business cycle, since funding needs should be greatest when there are many projects to finance.

On the benefit side, the availability of alternative sources of funding will affect the attractiveness of going public in many ways. At high levels of gearing, for example, a firm may find it increasingly expensive and difficult to raise bank loans, and may balk at the corporate control implications of tighter loan covenants or more intrusive bank monitoring. As the amount of retained earnings varies over the business cycle, a flotation therefore becomes increasingly tempting in an economic upswing, when earnings are still low. Regime changes, such as a reduction in capital gains taxes or a more liberal attitude to the tax deductibility of going-public-related costs, will also increase the net benefit the original owners receive from a flotation.

The available evidence generally supports these considerations. Högholm and Rydqvist (forthcoming) link the European 'IPO boom' of the 1980s to rising share prices and deregulation, while Ljungqvist (1995b) provides evidence that in Germany the number of flotations changes over time in line with the business cycle, stock market conditions, and the gradual increase in competitiveness of the underwriter market.

2.3.2 Predictability of underpricing

Like IPO volume, the extent of underpricing also tends to vary over time in most markets, as the graphs in Figure 2.4 illustrate. In many countries, the profitability of a stagging strategy—subscribing indiscriminately to all IPOs and selling as soon as trading commences—

would generally have been much higher in the early to mid-1980s than in the late 1980s and early 1990s. Rarely, however, were new issues overpriced on an annual average, which points to the relatively low risk a stag would have faced.

What is more striking, though, is the relatively high persistence in initial returns. Periods of high initial returns—sometimes called 'hot issue' markets—frequently last for several months, which suggests that underpricing is highly positively auto-correlated.[5] From the stag's point of view this is good news, since it implies that future (average) initial returns are predictable with a considerable degree of accuracy. To the economist, it presents a challenge: if underpricing is worrying *per se* from an efficient markets point of view, its predictability is even more worrying since it implies that a yet more profitable trading rule than *indiscriminate* stagging exists.

Fig. 2.4. Underpricing of IPOs in selected countries, 1960–1994

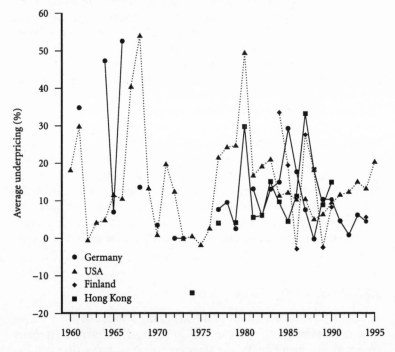

[5] For US evidence on this, see Ibbotson, Ritter, and Sindelar (1994).

Forecasts of future initial returns can be made considerably more precise if factors other than past underpricing are considered. There is overwhelming evidence that underpricing is higher in buoyant stock markets: Davis and Yeomans (1976) (UK), Reilly (1977) (USA), McGuinness (1992) (Hong Kong), and Rydqvist (1993) (Sweden) all show that initial returns tend to be higher following periods of high returns on the market index. In Germany, IPOs are more heavily underpriced not only when the market is performing well, but also in macroeconomic upswings, when already-listed firms issue historically large amounts of seasoned equity, and when stock market volatility is low.

Explanations for the link between the incidence of 'hot issue' periods and stock market and business cycle conditions are much thinner on the ground. Conceptually, the magnitude of initial returns will vary when the fundamental parameters identified in theoretical underpricing models change. For instance, if underpricing serves to insure against litigation, greater underpricing will become necessary as the likelihood of future lawsuits increases. However, there is as yet no convincing effort to endogenize how and why these parameters change with macroeconomic and stock market conditions: why, for instance, would litigation risk increase in buoyant markets?

Another approach is to argue that, as the costs of going public are lower and the benefits greater in certain periods, a flotation could become so attractive that a firm would be willing to accept higher than usual underpricing in order to take advantage of a good IPO climate. This takes us back to the earlier discussion of cycles in IPO volume: buoyant stock markets and economic upswings are good times to go public and hence may induce a greater tolerance of underpricing.

An alternative explanation, favoured by investment bankers, relates to the availability of funds. When a particularly large number of companies tap the equity market, as for instance when there are a large number of privatization offers, a greater enticement in the form of underpricing must be offered for investors to be willing to subscribe for shares. However, this rings somewhat hollow. Most developed economies should be assumed to have deep enough financial markets to absorb large amounts of new stock on a bait of, say, a 'mere' 10 per cent underpricing discount. In emerging markets, the often enormous over-subscription ratios—factors of 100 and more are not uncommon in Asia—even in times of heavy IPO activity indicate that investors would be more than willing to buy even if offer prices were set higher.

It thus seems unlikely that the supply of investable funds is highly sensitive to the number of offerings.

2.3.3 Underpricing as a leading indicator of IPO activity

Typically, the underpricing and IPO volume cycles are not perfectly synchronized. Rather, 'hot issue' markets seem to be followed by periods of high new issue volume, as in the USA, where Ibbotson, Ritter, and Sindelar (1994) document that initial returns lead volume by 6–12 months. A similar lead–lag relationship is evident in Australia (Lee, Taylor and Walter 1994) as well as in Germany and Sweden (Ljungqvist 1995b).

Why more companies go public after periods of sustained underpricing is not yet clear. However, it is possible that higher underpricing acts as a signal of investors' appetite for new offerings, and thus entices firms to go public. Alternatively, firms seen to be going public despite a high underpricing cost may signal to other companies that now is a good time to float, in terms of the fundamental cost–benefit trade-off referred to earlier. Or it may become easier to benchmark an underwriter's marketing effort—which must be higher the higher the offer price—and hence to negotiate a keener offer price as the information set increases over the IPO volume cycle: at the peak of an IPO wave, it may be very hard for an underwriter to use the justification that the market is hostile to flotations when arguing for a lower issue price.

2.4 Long-Run Performance and the 'New Equity Puzzle'

2.4.1 The evidence

Implicit in the underpricing literature traditionally has been an investment strategy which assumes that the subscriber sells her allotted shares in the early after-market, thus profiting from the discount at which the shares were offered. A natural question to ask is how those investors fare who buy from the initial subscribers when trading starts. The efficient markets hypothesis would suggest that IPOs perform neutrally, in accordance with asset pricing theories, thus yielding neither abnormal profits nor excess losses. Early studies investigated this question by looking at the first few months of trading of IPOs. The fact that no abnormal performance could be detected was construed as evidence that the stock market efficiently values IPO shares once trading begins, and that no further abnormal returns—beyond the underpricing premium—can be earned.

However, a seminal study by Ritter (1991) found evidence of substantial negative abnormal returns over longer time horizons: a comprehensive sample of 1,526 US companies that came to market between 1975 and 1984 underperformed a matching-firm index by some 29 per cent after three years of trading. That this is not a recent phenomenon can clearly be seen in Table 2.2: even in the 1920s American IPOs underperformed the market. Nor is it confined to the USA: with the notable exceptions of Korea and Sweden, work in other countries has shown that long-run market-adjusted returns, typically measured over a three-year investment horizon, are negative, with first-day buyers faring particularly badly in Australia, Brazil, and Canada. Thus, while new issues are a profitable investment opportunity if bought at flotation, they should not be held long beyond the first few weeks or months of trading, and if possible should be shorted to profit from the negative return drift.

Astonishingly, seasoned equity offerings (SEOs) share the poor long-term performance of IPOs: Loughran and Ritter (1995) and Affleck-Graves and Spiess (1995) both document wealth losses—of a similar magnitude to those experienced in IPOs—over three- and five-year holding periods in large samples of US seasoned equity issues. Levis (forthcoming) reports a similar pattern for the UK. Since newly listed companies have a high propensity to return to the primary market within a few years of going public, IPO firms are over-represented in any SEO sample. One might, therefore, suspect that the poor performance of firms issuing seasoned equity may be driven by the IPO underperformance phenomenon. However, it turns out that long-seasoned firms underperform by just as much as recent IPOs, following an issue of common shares. Hence poor post-issue performance seems to afflict both firms that have recently gone public and those that have been trading for a long time. Moreover, Ikenberry, Lakonishok, and Vermaelen (1995) document the mirror image of issuing firms' underperformance for companies repurchasing their own shares: buybacks are followed by several years of outperforming the market.

Studies focusing on long-run operating performance confirm the results found in share price studies. Jain and Kini (1994) report significant declines in operating returns on assets, as well as operating cash flows deflated by total assets, over the first three to five years after

Table 2.2. Comparative evidence of IPO long-run performance

Country	Study	Sample period	Sample size	Window (years)[a]	Return (%)[b]
Australia	Lee *et al.* (1994)	1976–89	266	3	−51.0
Brazil	Aggarwal *et al.* (1993)	1980–90	62	3	−47.0
Canada	Shaw (1971)	1956–63	105	5	−32.3
Chile	Aggarwal *et al.* (1993)	1982–90	28	3	−23.7
Finland	Keloharju (1993*b*)	1984–89	79	3	−21.1
Germany	Ljungqvist (1996*b*)	1970–90	145	3	−12.1
Great Britain	Levis (1993*a*)	1980–88	712	3	−8.1
Hong Kong	McGuinness (1993*b*)	1980–90	72	2	−18.3
Japan	Cai and Wei (1996)	1971–90	172	3	−27.0
Korea	Kim *et al.* (1995)	1985–88	99	3	+91.6
Singapore	Hin and Mahmood (1993)	1976–84	45	3	−9.2
Sweden	Loughran *et al.* (1994)	1980–90	162	3	+1.2
Switzerland	Kunz and Aggarwal (1994)	1983–89	34	3	−6.1
USA	Stigler (1964*a,b*)	1923–28	70	5	−37.7
USA	Simon (1989)[c]	1926–33	35	5	−39.0
USA	Simon (1989)[d]	1934–40	20	5	+6.2
USA	Stigler (1964*a,b*)	1949–55	46	5	−25.1
USA	Cusatis *et al.* (1993)[e]	1965–88	146	3	+33.6
USA	Loughran (1993)	1967–87	3656	6	−33.3
USA	Loughran and Ritter (1995)	1970–90	4753	5	−30.0
USA	Ritter (1991)	1975–84	1526	3	−29.1

[a] Window is the number of years over which after-market returns are recorded.

[b] Returns are calculated over the investment window and thus are not annualized, exclude the initial underpricing return, and are generally market-adjusted, but not risk-adjusted. Some authors use a range of benchmarks; in these cases, a representative result is shown. Computation methodologies vary.

[c] IPOs on regional exchanges only; a sample of 18 NYSE stocks performed neutrally (average cumulative abnormal return: −1.16 per cent after 5 years).

[d] Aggregated NYSE and non-NYSE long-run IPO returns, reported in Simon's (1989) table B4.

[e] Subsidiaries of listed companies that were spun off in an initial public offering. The positive returns are driven by a subsample of spin-offs which were targets of takeover bids.

flotation among a large sample of US IPOs, both in absolute terms and relative to a matched control sample. Again, the same pattern holds for seasoned equity offerings: according to Loughran and Ritter (1994), operating performance peaks at about the time of the offering and declines significantly over the following four years, relative to a matched control sample of non-issuers. Once more, this is not driven by the subset of recent IPO firms that reissue. Summarizing these various phenomena, Loughran and Ritter (1995) label the poor operating and share price performance of firms that go public or issue seasoned equity the 'new equity puzzle'.

2.4.2 Theoretical explanations

Equilibrium explanations for this curious evidence are less than abundant. The very existence of profitable trading rules, which is implied by the systematic long-run underperformance of new equity issues, suggests a potential violation of the informational efficiency of stock markets and thus continues to defy theoretical modelling efforts based on the paradigm of rational behaviour.

However, there are some simple interpretations. First, it is possible that the widespread practice by underwriters of supporting an issue's trading price in the after-market spuriously leads to observations of abnormally low returns: flotations that are initially supported might well underperform if measured from the first trading day—when prices are artificially high—but would perform neutrally if measured from the date when support is withdrawn. Second, it is difficult at the best of times to control correctly for risk over long time horizons. The problems are more daunting in the case of IPOs since, owing to the automatic absence of pre-flotation share prices, no simple estimates of systematic risk are available. Hence the available evidence should probably be taken with a pinch of salt: maybe the poor returns are less marked if adjusted for true risk.

While the possibility therefore remains that market microstructure or imperfect benchmarking lies behind the poor returns, most of the literature has instead focused on fads and irrational investor behaviour. A typical argument runs like this. The evidence on operating performance indicates that firms go public after periods of fast growth in earnings that are not sustained post-flotation; in fact, there is some evidence suggesting that companies even massage their accounts prior to going public. Investors then pay over the odds when trading starts—thus leading to first-day underpricing price jumps—but are consistently surprised by the decline in operating performance and therefore mark down share prices in response to worse-than-expected earnings reports—thus leading to negative after-market returns.

A variation on this theme suggests that investors are only periodically (rather than permanently) over-optimistic about the prospects of firms coming to market. If companies could 'time' their flotations to coincide with periods of faddishly high expectations among investors, we would at once have an explanation not only for the long-run under-performance, but also for the clustering of IPO volume: firms are simply taking advantage of windows of opportunity.

However, to us it seems unlikely that investors can be consistently fooled in this manner. Any explanation that is predicated on persistent misvaluation raises as many questions as it purports to answer: above all, why do investors not learn from past experience? After all, IPOs seem to have been performing poorly for many decades, at least in the USA, so one would reasonably expect investors to discount glowing earnings reports when deciding how much to pay for newly floated shares. Moreover, the 'timing' argument rests on the unrealistic assumption that firms can tell when investors are excessively optimistic: surely, if they could, they would not merely go public but instead would go short on equities, wait until investor sentiment had returned to normal, then cover their short positions and make an enormous arbitrage profit in the process.

In summary, while the air is thick with conjecture, economists do not yet know what causes initial public offerings to perform poorly in the long run. The evidence, if correct, is disturbing. With initial under-pricing, at least there is an element of arbitrariness in setting the offer price, and thus we can think of reasons why one might want to set the price below its expected after-market value. But for a certain type of firm (those recently listed) to perform worse than expected consistently and persistently, something must be amiss either with the way we measure risk and performance, or with the asset pricing theories we use to form expected returns, or with the rationality of market participants.

2.5 Summary

Since the early 1980s, initial public offerings have enjoyed increasing popularity in many economies which have not traditionally relied much on public equity markets for the funding needs of their corporate sector. Almost without exception, these countries have experienced the same empirical phenomena to which the more developed Anglo-

Saxon primary markets have long been prone: flotations are significantly underpriced initially but seem to perform poorly over the first few years of trading. These stylized facts of initial underpricing and long-run underperformance, and to a lesser extent the time series behaviour of initial returns and IPO volume, have for some time occupied a central place on the theoretical and empirical research agenda, and this book is devoted to assessing the state of this literature.

While few countries have escaped an underpricing study, less hard evidence is available about the long-run performance of newly floated firms. The United States apart, most studies look at relatively short and recent sampling periods, concentrating mostly on the 1980s. There is thus a great need for further international research to assess the robustness of the extant findings, with respect to both different countries and other sampling periods. Germany, for instance, had a lively IPO market before the Wars—did these flotations underperform as well?

The long-run performance evidence is still exploratory also in another respect. Not knowing what the true expected return on a stock should be, researchers resort to asserting certain benchmarks, for instance using asset pricing models such as the CAPM or the Fama-French (1992) three-factor model. Should the observed return turn out to be lower than the derived expectation, the firm is deemed to underperform. Obviously, this procedure is only as good as the benchmark one uses—a choice which in the case of IPOs is made more difficult in a number of ways: how to estimate systematic risk when there is no pre-flotation share price history? what benchmark to use if, as in Finland, twice as many firms have gone public as were initially listed? It is entirely possible that the resolution of these methodological issues will eventually be sufficient to explain the apparently anomalous share price behaviour. For the moment, however, we will accept the evidence at face value.

What is astonishing is that underpricing and long-run underperformance are such consistent phenomena across countries with very different company populations, corporate control mechanisms ('bank-based' v. 'market-based'), and institutional, legal, taxation, regulatory, historical, and cultural frameworks. This calls for theoretical explanations that are equally applicable to any country whose IPOs experience abnormal performance, whatever its particular framework.

Few, if any, available theoretical models fit this bill. Most are phrased with the US new issue market in mind, but various features of the US framework purportedly driving the results are conspicuously absent in other countries. The next part of this book will outline the main theoretical explanations that have been advanced in the academic literature, evaluate them against the available evidence, and discuss their general applicability in the light of cross-country institutional differences. Despite a multitude of models, we feel that no single explanation can claim universal acceptance, and that some of the more popular models sound less than plausible once one looks beyond US horizons.

The final part of the book draws theory and evidence together in an attempt to derive two types of policy conclusions: how best to privatize state-owned firms, and how best to structure the primary market function of a stock market.

Part II

THEORY AND EVIDENCE

The purpose of this survey is threefold: to bring out the salient features of various models which attempt to explain the stylized facts reviewed in the previous chapter; to give an overview of the empirical evidence regarding these models; and to discuss the applicability of these explanations in the light of international differences in institutional and other conditions. No integrative survey exists so far of the IPO literature, with the result that considerable research effort is still being expended in areas that we would view as unfruitful in the light of both testing evidence and cross-country differences in key conditions.

Attempts to explain underpricing fall into three broad categories: (i) theories focusing on the informational asymmetries among the three main parties to an IPO: the issuing firm, the underwriting or sponsoring investment bank, and investors; (ii) institutional explanations; and (iii) corporate ownership and control considerations. Chapters 3, 4 and 5 will discuss these three categories in turn. Chapter 6 will turn to the most recently discovered stylized fact, the tendency of new issues to underperform in the long run. Ideally, it should be possible to explain both underpricing and long-term underperformance in a unified framework, but as the chapter will show the two phenomena are particularly difficult to reconcile within conventional underpricing models. The two modelling approaches that have succeeded in uniting the two phenomena are the 'fads' and price support literatures, which have in common the view that first-day trading prices do not correctly value the flotation, making a subsequent price correction inevitable. The burgeoning statistical literature on risk mis-measurement and the robustness of statistical testing procedures will also be discussed.

While the theoretical literature has risen to the challenge of explaining the underpricing phenomenon, it has been less successful at rationalizing the regularities in the time series patterns of initial returns and IPO volume. Most underpricing models can be made consistent with cyclicality in underpricing if their underlying parameters are allowed to vary over time, although empirically it seems doubtful whether the variance in these parameters is sufficiently large. We are thus left without any compelling explanation for the predictable time variation in IPO volume and underpricing returns.

3

ASYMMETRIC INFORMATION

....

3.1 Adverse Selection Models: The Winner's Curse

Perhaps the best-known asymmetric information model of initial underpricing is Rock's (1986) winner's curse. Rock assumes that both the issuing firm and its underwriting bank are completely uninformed about the true value of the shares on offer, whereas some—but not all—investors are perfectly informed. To justify these assumptions, he alludes to the notion that the market in the aggregate has better information than any one player, including the issuer itself. Since issuer and bank are assumed to have the same information, the model also abstracts from agency problems: the bank acts in the firm's best interest. Given the presence of informed investors, uninformed investors face a winner's curse: they stand a greater chance of being allocated stock in overpriced rather than in rationed underpriced flotations, the reason being that informed investors avoid subscribing to IPOs they expect to be overpriced. For an uninformed investor, therefore, receiving a large allocation is bad news, which will tend to reduce her willingness to subscribe for shares in the first place.

If, as Rock further assumes, the primary market is dependent on the continued participation of uninformed investors, in the sense that informed demand is insufficient to take up all shares on offer even in lucrative flotations, something needs to be done to keep the uninformed in the market. The solution is underpricing: underwriters enforce an underpricing equilibrium that compensates the uninformed for the allocation bias and the informed for their information production. Note that it is not rationing *per se* that necessitates underpricing; it is instead the bias in rationing, with expected conditional allocation probabilities being smaller in good than in bad offerings. This is a variation on Akerlof's (1970) lemon's problem in the used car market: uninformed buyers will withdraw from a market if their informational disadvantage results in their being presented with an adverse selection from the quality distribution of goods.

Going public is, for the most part, a one-off event in a firm's history. Dynamically, the primary market is under threat from Rock's winner's curse, but no individual firm gains much from contributing to its continued viability when coming to market. This leads to a free-rider problem: collectively, all current and future issuers benefit from a reduction in the winner's curse, but, because part of the benefit from underpricing accrues to other issuers, firms individually have a suboptimal incentive to underprice. Indeed, it would be individually optimal to let someone else bribe uninformed investors into the market but overprice one's own flotation. Enter the underwriters: as repeat players, banks do have an incentive to ensure that new issues are underpriced lest they lose underwriting commissions in the future, as Beatty and Ritter (1986) show. Banks' activities are kept in check by the vigilance of issuers on the one hand and investors on the other: underwriters that underprice too much (too little) should subsequently lose business from issuers (investors).

3.1.1 Testable implications and evidence

Implicit in the winner's curse model is the notion that, if properly adjusted for rationing, uninformed investors' abnormal underpricing returns tend to the riskless rate, on average—that is, just enough to ensure their continued participation in the market (cf. Table 3.1, which lists the testable implications of the winner's curse model alongside the available empirical evidence). Similarly, the informed investors' conditional underpricing return should just provide a normal return on their information production. While the former is potentially testable, the latter is not, not least because informed and uninformed investors cannot in practice be told apart. Moreover, very few markets publish enough allocation data to allow underpricing returns to be adjusted for rationing. The evidence here is mixed: while Singapore, the UK and Finland do indeed see initial returns reduced to zero when adjusted for rationing, there are many more countries—Hong Kong and Germany, to name but two—either where this is not the case or where there simply are no overpriced issues and thus no allocation bias for the uninformed, at least *ex post*.

As underpricing represents an involuntary cost to the issuer, there

Table 3.1. The winner's curse explanation of IPO underpricing

Result	Source	Empirical evidence
1 In order to avoid the 'lemons' problem of adverse selection, issuers rationally underprice, in an informational environment in which • some investors are perfectly informed; • all other investors, issuers, and underwriters have no information about 'true' firm value. Underpricing returns then tend to the riskless rate when ration-adjusted.	Rock (1986) Beatty and Ritter (1986)	Yes: Koh and Walter (1989) [Singapore] Levis (1990) [UK] Keloharju (1993b) [Finland] No: McGuinness (1993a) [Hong Kong] Cheung et al. (1993) [Hong Kong]
2 Underpricing decreases as heterogeneity of information decreases (e.g. in offerings geared towards 'informed' investors, usually assumed to be institutional investors).	Michaely and Shaw (1994)	Yes: Michaely and Shaw (1994) [USA] No: Jenkinson (1990) [UK] Tinic (1988) [USA]
3 To cut the underpricing cost, the informational asymmetry can be reduced by choosing a reputable underwriter (signalling and certification): more prestigious underwriters • are associated with less risky IPOs; • thus underprice less in expectation.	Carter and Manaster (1990) Booth and Smith (1986)	Yes: Carter and Manaster (1990) [USA] Johnson and Miller (1988) [USA] Michaely and Shaw (1994) [USA] La Chapelle and Neuberger (1983) [USA] Kim et al. (1993) [Korea] No: James and Wier (1990) [USA] McGuinness (1992) [Hong Kong] Ljungqvist (1995a) [Germany]

Table 3.1. (*cont.*)

Result	Source	Empirical evidence	
3' *ditto* for other agents	Titman and Trueman (1986)	Yes: Barry *et al.* (1990)	[USA]
		Megginson and Weiss (1991)	[USA]
		venture capitalists	
		Balvers *et al.* (1988)	[USA]
		Beatty (1989)	[USA]
		auditors	
		No: McGuinness (1992)	[Hong Kong]
		auditors	
4 Underwriters who underprice too much (little) will lose business from issuers (investors).	Beatty and Ritter (1986)	Yes: Beatty and Ritter (1986)	[USA]
		James (1992)	[USA]
5 Underpricing is greater when the underwriter exercises the 'over-allotment option' (to issue up to 15% more stock).	Rock (1986)		
6 'Hot issue' periods are characterised by a higher level of *ex ante* uncertainty necessitating higher underpricing.	Ritter (1984)	No: Ritter (1984)	[USA]
7 The greater is *ex ante* uncertainty, the higher is expected underpricing.	Ritter (1984) Beatty and Ritter (1986)	See Table 3.2.	

are clear incentives to reduce the information asymmetry and the resulting adverse selection problem between informed and uninformed investors. One solution is to market a flotation solely to one or the other of these categories, but not to both. This typically happens in UK private placings—where brokers contact only their regular (institutional) investors; interestingly, however, these are no less underpriced than offers sold to the public at large. Another way to reduce the asymmetry in information is to retain a reputable underwriter (or other agent, such as auditor); by agreeing to sponsor an offering, the prestigious intermediary certifies the quality of the issue. If reputation capital is valuable, prestigious banks will refrain from underwriting low-quality issuers. The information content of the firm's choice of intermediaries may therefore reduce investors' incentives to produce their own information, which in turn will mitigate against the winner's curse. Broadly speaking, this certification hypothesis seems to hold in the USA, but not in some other countries (cf. Table 3.1).

A key empirical implication, due to Ritter (1984) and formalized in Beatty and Ritter (1986), is that underpricing should increase in the *ex ante* uncertainty surrounding an issue. Beatty and Ritter provide an interesting intuition for this result. An investor who decides to engage in information production implicitly invests in a call option on the IPO, which she will exercise if the 'true' price exceeds the strike price, the price at which the shares are offered to the public. The value of this option increases in the extent of uncertainty, so more investors will become informed. This raises the required underpricing, since an increase in the number of informed traders aggravates the winner's curse problem—although, of course, if enough people become informed, the winner's curse would presumably disappear.

Table 3.2 lists the various studies that have looked at the relationship between numerous proxies for *ex ante* uncertainty and initial underpricing. Even though the hypothesis receives overwhelming support, the fact that almost every underpricing theory worth its salt also predicts a positive relationship between risk and return (see below) renders it unsuitable as evidence in favour of Rock's model. It can be used as an indirect test, however. Ritter (1984), in trying to square underpricing cycles with the winner's curse, argues that, if the winner's curse is the sole reason why IPOs are underpriced, then changes in the extent of the winner's curse—say, arising from changes in *ex ante* uncertainty—should be the sole reason why underpricing varies over time. However, he finds that it is industry-specific events, rather than

Table 3.2. Evidence on the relationship between *ex ante* uncertainty and underpricing

Result and study	Country	Proxy
Yes: Beatty and Ritter (1986)	USA	log (1 + number of uses of IPO proceeds)
Beatty and Ritter (1986) Ljungqvist (1996*b*)	USA Germany	Inverse gross proceeds
Ritter (1984)	USA	Heteroscedasticity (variance increases in size of underpricing discounts)
		Variables such as age and sales (showing how established the firm is)
Ritter (1984) Wasserfallen and Wittleder (1994) Clarkson and Merkley (1994) Finn and Higham (1988)	USA Germany Canada Australia	Standard deviation of daily after-market returns
Miller and Reilly (1987) Göppl and Sauer (1990)	USA Germany	Daily trade volume in early after-market
Muscarella and Vetsuypens (1989*b*)	USA	Relistings *v.* truly new listings
James and Wier (1990)	USA	Certification role for established credit relationships
Slovin and Young (1990)	USA	Monitoring role in bank lending relationships
Clarkson and Merkley (1994)	Canada	Is earnings forecast included in prospectus?
Ritter (1991)	USA	Age
No: Muscarella and Vetsuypens (1989*b*)	USA	Within group of relistings: those that were listed as a whole not significantly less underpriced than those listed only as a subsidiary
McGuinness (1992)	Hong Kong	log (1 + number of uses of IPO proceeds)
		Gross proceeds

Note: Most underpricing models predict that, the greater is *ex ante* uncertainty about the 'true' value of an initial public offering, the higher must be underpricing. The table summarizes the international evidence on this proposition for a variety of uncertainty proxies.

changes in the risk composition of IPO cohorts, that drive changes in initial returns.

3.1.2 Discussion

While the winner's curse model rests on a deceptively simple and rather intuitive observation—that more heavily underpriced flotations will be more heavily rationed, making a mockery of simple measures of underpricing which are based on an equally weighted average—there are some serious grounds for scepticism. How realistic is the assumption that issuers must pay for the uninformed investors' participation in an offering? If, as Rock asserts, the resources of the informed are limited, the uninformed could simply invest through the informed investors, in exchange for a fee, to avoid the mistake of subscribing to overpriced issues. This is one of the reasons why investment funds exist in the first place: there are economies of scale in becoming informed.

How severe is the allocation bias in practice? The answer depends on who is informed and who is not, a distinction that mostly defies empirical testing. Several studies have looked at institutional versus retail investors. Needless to say, we cannot rule out that the information asymmetry is most severe *within* groups, rather than between institutionals and retail investors.[1] Nevertheless, this approach has yielded some interesting insights. The Securities and Exchange Commission (1971) looked into the treatment of US institutional investors in stock market flotations. The findings are surprising: institutionals do *not* receive preferential treatment in the form of favourably sized allocations of oversubscribed issues; on the contrary, oversubscribed issues are typically severely rationed. Since information production is undoubtedly costly, would the rather small per-firm allocations really justify becoming informed? More recent evidence by Weiss Hanley and Wilhelm (1995) extends this observation: no doubt institutionals benefit greatly from underpriced IPOs, but remarkably, there is no difference in the size of allocations institutionals receive in underpriced and overpriced issues.

---

[1] Are institutional investors informed? If they are, they ought to be able to invest selectively in better-performing IPOs. While Weiss Hanley and Wilhelm (1995) can find no evidence in support of this conjecture, Field (1995) shows that IPO firms perform better relative to matched seasoned firms, the greater their institutional shareholdings. However, this does not prove institutionals are informed: even the flotations with greatest institutional stakes underperform broad stock market indices. Underperformance in Japan is unrelated to shareholder structure (Cai and Wei 1996).

This finding is significant in two respects. First, it suggests that institutionals cannot engage in 'cream-skimming', that is using their information advantage to avoid overpriced flotations. Second, institutionals do not impose a winner's curse on retail investors. Later in this chapter we will discuss a model due to Benveniste and Spindt (1989), which accurately predicts that institutionals cannot refuse to participate in less attractive offerings, as the underwriters would strike them off their distribution lists in future IPOs. Again, doubters may point to the unobserved distribution of information across and within these investor categories; but in our view, at least a modicum of doubt regarding the winner's curse is appropriate.

Underpricing theories essentially come in one of two forms: either underpricing is thought to be the involuntary but necessary response to some underlying information or other problem, or it is regarded as a deliberate action chosen by the issuing firm in the pursuit of some wealth-maximizing objective. As the winner's curse model falls into the former category, one would expect firms to be keen on any change to the allocation mechanism which takes account of the private information among investors and thus necessitates no (or lower) underpricing. The most notable example of such an alternative mechanism is the tender offer. Yet tender offers have proved unpopular with issuers in countries where there is a choice of offering method, as mentioned in Chapter 2.[2] This implies that underpricing is not necessarily as involuntary as the winner's curse suggests. We next turn to a theory that ascribes a value to underpricing.

3.2 Underpricing as a Signal of Firm Quality

Another strand of the theoretical literature reverses Rock's assumption regarding the informational asymmetry between issuing firms and investors. If companies have better information about the present value and risk of their future cash flows than do investors, underpricing may become a means of convincing potential buyers of the high 'true' value of the firm. Allen and Faulhaber (1989), Grinblatt and

---

[2] Wimmers (1988) reports survey evidence that 76 per cent of his respondents (German IPO firms in 1978–87) would not have wished to use a tender instead of a fixed-price offering. Tenders seem to have disappeared altogether in the UK since 1986, cf. Jenkinson (1990). For similar evidence from the Netherlands, cf. Wessels (1989).

Hwang (1989), and Welch (1989, 1996) have contributed theories with this feature. These models are variations on the signalling theme first introduced into economics by Spence (1974) in the context of labour markets. In this section, we will first discuss the workings of signalling in general, then show how signalling might work in the IPO context in particular, and last consider the testable implications and empirical evidence.

3.2.1 Signalling models

In a signalling model, one party has incomplete information about another party's unobserved characteristics. For instance, Spence has workers being better informed about their own ability than are employers. Because of the obvious incentives to lie, the informed party (the sender) cannot simply announce her type but rather must take some action to signal it—in the spirit of 'actions speak louder than words'. The uninformed party (the receiver) then transacts with the sender, making the terms of transaction depend on the observed signal. For instance, employers might offer a wage contract which depends on a worker's education level.

In general, there are two alternative equilibria: pooling and separating equilibria. In a pooling equilibrium, all types send the same signal, so the receiver cannot infer the unobserved characteristic and thus cannot distinguish between the various types of informed parties. In Spence's model, every worker is paid the expected marginal product, implying that high-ability workers are underpaid and low-ability ones are overpaid. In a separating equilibrium, on the other hand, different types send different signals, on the basis of which the receiver can tell them apart. For instance, higher-ability workers signal their type by choosing a higher level of education, allowing employers to offer well-educated workers a higher wage.

For a separating equilibrium to exist, (i) there must be signalling costs which (ii) differ across types.[3] Consider Spence's labour example. In a separating equilibrium, low-ability workers have a clear incentive to mimic high-ability workers, as this would raise their pay. For a separating equilibrium to come about, therefore, it must be incentive-compatible for the low-ability workers not to adopt the high-ability workers' choice of signal, which will be the case if the signal is costlier,

---

[3] These two conditions form what is called the *single-crossing property*.

at the margin, for low-ability than for high-ability workers. By the same token, high-ability types will choose to separate only if the associated cost is outweighed by the benefit, i.e. the higher wage rate. So, there are two incentive-compatibility constraints. If they are not met, a pooling equilibrium will result.[4]

It is a feature of separating equilibria that the type that is forced to signal is strictly worse off than in a first-best full-information world (or if her type could credibly and verifiably be announced). This is because—while she *will* receive the fair terms of transaction conditional upon the signal fully revealing her type, as she would in the absence of the informational asymmetry—she has to engage in costly signalling. Low types, on the other hand, receive the same benefit as they would in a first-best world, while not incurring the signalling cost.

The required ingredients of a signalling model thus are: differential signalling cost and a mechanism for reaping the benefit of the costly signal.

3.2.2 Signalling with underpricing

The differences between the IPO signalling models are fewer than the similarities. The key informational assumption states that the issuing firm is better informed about the present value of its future cash flows than are investors or underwriters (the latter not having any explicit role in these models). Another key but hidden assumption is that firms go public in order to transfer ownership and control fully to new shareholders—which may not necessarily be the case in reality. Under this assumption, entrepreneurs are assumed to maximize the expected proceeds (or expected utility of the proceeds) of a two-stage sale: they sell a fraction α of the firm at flotation and the remainder in a later open market sale.

Signalling true value is beneficial to a high-value company as it allows a higher price to be fetched at the second-stage sale if separation is achieved. In the words of Ibbotson (1975), who is credited with the original intuition for the IPO signalling literature, issuers underprice in order to 'leave a good taste in investors' mouths'. With some positive probability, a firm's true type is revealed before the post-IPO financing stage, introducing the risk to low-quality issuers that any cheating on

---

[4] In addition, there are also two participation constraints, stating that in equilibrium each party has to be at least as well off as it would be if it withdrew from the market.

their part will be detected before they can reap the benefit from the signal. This makes separation possible, in that it decreases the expected benefit from signalling to low-value firms and thus drives a wedge between high-value and low-value firms' marginal signalling cost.

The signal is the initial offering price. Provided the implied reduction in IPO proceeds and the risk of detection are sufficiently great to deter low-value firms from mimicking high-value ones, by floating at a lower price and thus underpricing, a high-value firm can influence investors' after-market beliefs about its value which in turn determine the amount raised in the final sell-off. High-value firms thus face a trade-off between costly signalling and greater subsequent proceeds.

While the signalling models are *consistent* with 'hot issue' periods if some exogenous shock changes the fundamental parameters, thus causing many firms simultaneously to switch from a pooling to an underpricing equilibrium, we see no economically compelling reason why the costs of or benefits from signalling should change much over time. Moreover, because the required switch would be exogenous to the model, the signalling literature can shed no light on *why* 'hot issue' markets might occur.

Table 3.3 summarizes the key differences between the three pioneering IPO signalling models by Allen and Faulhaber (1989), Grinblatt and Hwang (1989), and Welch (1989). Of these, Grinblatt and Hwang's is the richest. Here, investors are uncertain not only about the present value of the firms' future cash flows, but also about their variance. Risk-averse entrepreneurs therefore employ *two* signals—their retention rate and the level of underpricing—to signal these two unobservable attributes. The model generalizes Leland and Pyle's (1977) well-known insight that owners can reveal their knowledge of high future cash flows by retaining a larger fraction of equity in the firm, as the implied under-diversification is costlier to the owners of high-variance firms than to those of low-variance ones.

While the signalling models are technically elegant and perhaps intuitively appealing, there are several grounds for scepticism. Much depends on the empirical question whether companies do indeed follow two-stage selling strategies, as they must in signalling models in order to recoup the cost of the signal. And even if they do, the form that the second-stage financing round takes is important. In countries where shareholders enjoy pre-emptive rights to seasoned offerings of primary equity, there would be no benefit to signalling: it is a well-known fact that the pricing of a rights issue is wealth-neutral. Welch's

Table 3.3. A comparison of IPO signalling models

	Assumptions	Signal	Signalling cost	Benefit of signalling to high-value firms	Revelation of type
Allen and Faulhaber (1989)	2 firm types Risk-neutral firms	Initial offering price (P_0)	Forgone funds at IPO; cost greater to low-value firms	Owners sell remaining stake $(1-\alpha)$ in the after-market	Endogenous: Bayesian learning based on dividends which noisily reveal true type
Grinblatt and Hwang (1989)	Continuum of firm types Risk-averse entrepreneurs	Initial offering price and fraction of equity floated (P_0, α)	(i) Forgone funds at IPO (ii) Underdiversification	Owners later sell remaining stake $(1-\alpha)$ at a higher price and achieve portfolio diversification	Exogenous: nature may reveal type according to some probability
Welch (1989)		Initial offering price (P_0)	Direct imitation cost borne by low-value firms; if insufficient to deter mimicking, underpricing becomes additional wedge leading to separating equilibrium	Subsequent equity offering on behalf of the firm	Exogenous: nature may reveal type according to some probability

model, which relies on high-value firms separating to receive more favourable terms in subsequent equity offers, thus cannot account for the observed underpricing in Germany, the United Kingdom, and any other country whose investors enjoy pre-emptive rights.

Other countries require the original owners to abstain from selling further shares in the after-market for a specified period. For instance, the legal 'lock-in' period in the United States is 90 days, a minimum that issuers frequently voluntarily commit themselves to exceeding. The longer the 'lock-in' period, the greater the chance that exogenous events will come to dominate whatever goodwill the underpricing signal may have created initially.

The signalling models need to assume that IPO companies must meet some minimum capital requirement at flotation—otherwise, a firm could 'signal' by infinitely underpricing a single share, and subsequently raising its required funds in the after-market. The cost of such a signalling strategy would be zero, which would violate the single-crossing condition. The models were originally formulated with the US primary market in mind, where flotations typically concern young start-up companies. However, outside the USA and possibly the UK, issuers are mostly large, well-established firms which consequently do not conform to the minimum-capital assumption. Moreover, as discussed in Chapter 2, many European IPOs are primarily sell-outs by existing owners and managers, rather than capital-raising exercises by the firm. How sensible a minimum capital constraint is in the European context then depends on whether the original owners are sufficiently risk-averse to prefer a certain (since underwritten) amount of cash at flotation to an uncertain, but probably higher (since not underpriced) amount if selling into the after-market.

Finally, there is the question of optimal signalling: would firms really choose the underpricing signal if they had a wider menu of signals to choose from? Such a menu could include the choice of particularly reputable underwriters (Booth and Smith 1986), auditors (Titman and Trueman 1986), or venture capitalists, each of which would perform a certification-of-quality role; the quality of the board of directors and, in particular, the choice of non-executive directors; and managers' compensation structure. Unless underpricing proves to be the most cost-effective signal—which seems doubtful—the existence of alternatives dents the credibility of the signalling models.

In this context, it is worth mentioning a final variation on the signalling theme. Chemmanur's (1993) model of information production shares the informational and multiple-sale assumptions of the signalling literature, but does not view underpricing as an effective signalling device. Assume that none of the above signals—including underpricing—can bring about a separation equilibrium. In that case, high-quality issuers may attempt to tackle the root of the problem directly: the information asymmetry between themselves and market participants could be reduced by encouraging the latter to engage in information production about the firm. Underpricing is the compensation that high-quality firms offer to investors for their costly information production.

3.2.3 Testable implications and evidence

The models generate a rich set of empirical implications concerning the relationship between underpricing and the probability, size, speed, and announcement effect of subsequent equity sales. Table 3.4 lists the more important of these. Rather than discuss each of them in detail, we will focus on the generic (rather than model-specific) hypotheses which we deem most crucial to the credibility of the signalling approach.

If firms do underprice to condition investors favourably for later equity offerings, we would expect reissuing companies to have experienced greater underpricing. However, the evidence on this is mixed, as Table 3.4 shows: although supported in Finland and Hong Kong, this hypothesis is rejected in the USA—both for insider sales and primary equity offers. Nor is it true in general that more underpriced offerings increase the probability that a company will return to the market, except in Finland.

Clearly, signalling models would be of little practical importance if companies did *not* follow a multiple-stage sale policy of an initial flotation followed by subsequent equity offerings or insider sales. The evidence is hardly supportive. While Welch (1989) reports that about a quarter of US flotations in 1977–1982 returned to the market within three years of going public, raising significant amounts of money in relation to their IPO proceeds, the absence of a benchmark for what is a 'normal' level of equity issuance makes the interpretation of these figures difficult. Helwege and Liang (1996) provide quite different numbers. They track the 1983 IPO cohort in the USA and find that, in any of the following ten years, fewer than 4 per cent of firms return to the equity market: instead, the marked increase in investment

Table 3.4. The signalling explanation of IPO underpricing

Result	Source	Empirical evidence	
1 In order to signal firm quality so that they can subsequently issue seasoned equity or sell the owners' retained stakes at more favourable prices, high-quality issuers rationally underprice, in an informational environment in which • issuers are perfectly informed; • investors have no information about firm value. Therefore, companies that reissue have higher underpricing than those that do not.	Ibbotson (1975) Allen and Faulhaber (1989) Grinblatt and Hwang (1989) Welch (1989)	Yes: Keloharju (1993a) McGuinness (1992) No: Jenkinson (1990) Garfinkel (1993) James (1992) Michaely and Shaw (1992) Ruud (1990)	[Finland] [Hong Kong] [UK] [USA] [USA] [USA] [USA]
2 Companies for which there is no informational asymmetry, and thus no need to signal, do not underprice.	Allen and Faulhaber (1989)		
3 There is a positive relationship between underpricing and the probability of seasoned equity offering (SEO) or open-market insider sales.	Jegadeesh et al. (1993)	Yes: Keloharju (1993a) Jegadeesh et al. (1993) weak evidence No: Michaely and Shaw (1994) Garfinkel (1993) Levis (forthcoming)	[Finland] [USA] [USA] [USA] [UK]
4 There is a positive relationship between underpricing and the amount of SEO or open-	Welch (1989) Jegadeesh et al. (1993)	Yes: Jegadeesh et al. (1993) weak evidence	[USA]

Table 3.4. (*cont.*)

Result	Source	Empirical Evidence	
market insider sales. (Underpricing is costly, so high-quality firms minimize amount raised at IPO.)		No: Michaely and Shaw (1994) Keloharju (1993a)	[USA] [Finland]
5 There is a positive relationship between underpricing and the speed of SEO or open-market insider sales. (The higher underpricing, the shorter the interval between IPO and SEO.)	Jegadeesh *et al.* (1993)	Yes: Levis (forthcoming) Jegadeesh *et al.* (1993) *weak evidence* No: Keloharju (1993a)	[UK] [USA] [Finland]
5′ There is a negative relationship between underpricing and speed of SEO or open-market insider sales. (The higher underpricing, the longer the interval between IPO and SEO.)	Welch (1996)	Yes: Welch (1996)	[USA]
6 There is a less unfavourable price reaction to SEO announcement for firms with higher underpricing.	Welch (1989) Jegadeesh *et al.* (1993)	Yes: Jegadeesh *et al.* (1993) Slovin *et al.* (1994) *caveat*: the implied benefit at the SEO does not outweigh the under- pricing cost No: Michaely and Shaw (1994) Garfinkel (1993) Ruud (1990)	[USA] [USA] [USA] [USA] [USA]

7 There is a positive relationship between underpricing and subsequent earnings performance and dividend policy.	Allen and Faulhaber (1989)	No: Michaely and Shaw (1994)	[USA]
8 There is a more favourable price reaction to dividend announcements by firms that underprice more.	Allen and Faulhaber (1989)	No: Michaely and Shaw (1994)	[USA]
9 There is a positive relationship between underpricing and insider holdings for a given level of variance.	Grinblatt and Hwang (1989)	No: Michaely and Shaw (1994) James and Wier (1990)	[USA] [USA]
10 There is a positive relationship between underpricing and firm value for given fraction of insider holdings.	Grinblatt and Hwang (1989)	Yes: Koh et al. (1992) No: Michaely and Shaw (1994)	[Singapore] [USA]
11 There is a positive relationship between underpricing and firm value for given level of variance.	Grinblatt and Hwang (1989)	No: Michaely and Shaw (1994)	[USA]
12 There is a positive relationship between underpricing and post-issue operating performance.	Jain and Kini (1994)	No: Jain and Kini (1994)	[USA]
13 The greater ex ante uncertainty, the higher must be expected underpricing.	Grinblatt and Hwang (1989) Welch (1989)	See Table 3.2.	

expenditure that this cohort saw over its first decade of listing was financed mainly by retained earnings and private debt.

It is certainly true that these results, based as they are on observed outcomes, may fail to reflect companies' initial intentions at flotation and thus could be prone to bias. However, a third key implication receives no empirical support either. If underpricing does function as a signal of firm quality, subsequent cash flows should, on average, prove the signal right: whether or not it subsequently cashes in on the signal, the higher a company's underpricing, the higher its subsequent cash flows. Jain and Kini's (1994) study of post-flotation operating performance rejects this hypothesis.

The one implication that the evidence supports almost unequivocally is the positive relationship between *ex ante* uncertainty and initial returns, already familiar from the winner's curse. This relationship is implied by the models since a noisier environment increases the extent of underpricing that is necessary to achieve separation.

3.3 Principal–Agent Models

None of the models discussed so far has accorded investment banks any particular role. In the winner's curse model, bankers are assumed to be as ignorant about a firm's value as the firm itself, and in the signalling models banks are simply passive distributors of shares to the public. We now turn to a third set of models, which focuses on potential agency problems between the investment bank managing the flotation and the issuing firm. The scope for such problems seems immense: in many countries, the underwriter market is far from competitive, and the question arises whether banks have market power which they can exercise at the expense of issuers.

Even in a well-developed capital market such as in the USA, banks may be assumed to be better informed about investor demand than issuers. In an imperfectly competitive underwriter market, this may allow banks to earn information rents, for instance in the form of suboptimal selling effort. If effort is not perfectly observable or cannot be verified in court, banks find themselves in a moral hazard situation when acting as the issuers' agents in selling an IPO.

Conceptually, underwriters have conflicting incentives regarding the pricing of a flotation. On the one hand, underpricing lowers both the risk of failing to place all available stock with investors, and their unobservable effort costs in marketing and distributing an issue. On the other hand, since underwriting fees are typically proportional to gross flotation proceeds and thus inversely related to underpricing, investment banks should also have an incentive to minimize underpricing. It is conceivable that the resulting trade-off between underwriters' costs and benefits from underpricing involves some positive initial returns in equilibrium.

Baron and Holmström (1980) and Baron (1982) construct a screening model which focuses on the lead manager's benefit from underpricing. In a screening model, the uninformed party offers a menu or schedule of contracts, from which the informed party selects the one that is optimal given her unobserved type and/or hidden action. The contract schedule is designed to optimize the uninformed party's objective, which, given his informational disadvantage, will not be first-best optimal. An example is the various combinations of premium and excess a car insurer may offer in order to price-discriminate between different risks (unobservable type) or to induce safe driving (moral hazard).

To induce optimal use of the underwriter's superior information about investor demand, the issuer delegates the pricing decision to the bank: given her information, the underwriter self-selects a contract from a menu of combinations of IPO prices and underwriting spreads; if likely demand is low, she selects a high spread and a low price, and *vice versa* if demand is high.[5] This optimizes the agent's unobservable selling effort by making it dependent on market demand. Compared with the first-best solution under symmetric information, the second-best incentive-compatible contract involves underpricing in equilibrium, essentially since her informational advantage allows the agent to capture positive rents in the form of below-first-best effort costs. The more uncertain the value of the firm, the greater the asymmetry of information between issuer and underwriter, and thus the more valuable the latter's services become, resulting in greater underpricing. This is a further rationalization for the empirical observation that underpricing and proxies for *ex ante* uncertainty are positively related.

Models focusing on the role of underwriters are potentially very powerful in explaining the time variation in underpricing. The Baron–

---

[5] There is empirical support for the notion of a menu of compensation contracts. Dunbar (1995) shows that issuers successfully offer underwriters a menu that minimizes offering costs by inducing self-selection.

Table 3.5. The principal–agent explanation of IPO underpricing

Result	Source	Empirical evidence
1 In order to compensate underwriters for the use of their superior information, issuers rationally let underwriters underprice, in an informational environment in which • underwriters have superior information about demand for the new shares; and • their marketing efforts are unobservable/unverifiable.	Baron (1982) Baron and Holmström (1980)	No: Muscarella and Vetsuypens (1989a) [USA] *Banks underwriting own IPOs also underprice.* Barry et al. (1990) [USA] *Banks with equity stakes in firms also underprice.*
2 Self-marketed IPOs should be less underpriced, as there is no asymmetry of information.	Muscarella and Vetsuypens (1989a)	No: Muscarella and Vetsuypens (1989a) [USA]
3 The greater is *ex ante* uncertainty, the higher is expected underpricing.	Baron (1982)	See Table 3.2.
4 Larger offerings require greater distribution effort by the underwriter, and thus greater underpricing.	Michaely and Shaw (1994)	Yes: Michaely and Shaw (1994) [USA]

Holmström model implies non-stationary underpricing if the extent of informational asymmetry, and hence the level of agency costs, changes over time. For instance, an increase in competition may lower the scope for discretionary underpricing, by increasing the possibilities for yardstick competition or, more directly, via banks competing for mandates by offering higher flotation proceeds.

Table 3.5 outlines the model's testable hypotheses and the empirical evidence. A potentially powerful way to test the model would be to investigate the underpricing experience of flotations that have little or no informational asymmetry between issuer and bank, as when the underwriter has an equity stake in the company or the issuer cuts out the intermediary by going public without underwriting. Some limited evidence along these lines is available for the USA. Empirically, self-underwritten offerings are no less underpriced than traditional IPOs, a finding that, importantly, holds true for a set of self-underwritten bank offerings studied by Muscarella and Vetsuypens (1989a). It should be noted, though, that their results are based on very small sample sizes (38 banks), which cautions against drawing firm conclusions. Moreover, banks are not monolithic institutions, implying that there may still be inter-departmental moral hazard problems.

While the final judgement should, in our view, await further testing, the literature has, by and large, interpreted Muscarella and Vetsuypens's findings as a refutation of the Baron–Holmström model. Given the institutional and market power of banks in some countries—Germany being an obvious example—the model has immediate intuitive appeal in explaining the existence and evolution of underpricing, and thus, we feel, should not be abandoned lightly. A set of models that explore the role of intermediaries further will be discussed next.

3.4 Marketing and Institutional Constraints

3.4.1 Marketing

One of the main functions underwriters perform in many countries is marketing an issue to investors prior to the public offer. In the USA, underwriters conduct a so-called 'road show', where the company and its prospects are presented to selected—typically, institutional—investors. Having specified an initial price range, underwriters ask for non-binding 'indications of interest' (quantity bids) at various prices inside or, sometimes, outside the range. Ignoring for the moment problems of mis-reporting, banks can thereby glean information about the shape of the demand curve, which can be used in pricing and allocating an IPO.

With the increased popularity of book-building across much of Europe, this two-stage process of an information-gathering marketing phase followed by pricing and selling is now also common in, for example, the UK, Germany (since 1994), and Sweden (since the privatizations of the early 1990s). France, on the other, has so far bucked the book-building trend, relying instead for the most part on a single-stage, uniform-price, common-values auction, which cuts out the information-gathering stage.

The value of eliciting information stems from the plausible assumption that there are two dimensions of asymmetric information: first, firms have superior information about their own business situation, leading to the incentive to misrepresent familiar from signalling models; second, some investors are better informed about factors outside the firm's control, such as the prospects for competitors or the level of, and change in, the equity risk premium and cost of capital. The former asymmetry ensures that financial intermediaries have a valuable role to play in certifying the quality of an issue: with every IPO, an underwriter puts her reputation capital on the line, creating an incentive to market only high-quality firms to protect the long-term relationships she enjoys with core, informed investors. The latter asymmetry raises the question of truthful reporting: why should investors reveal any positive information they might have? After all, by not disclosing their information, they could subscribe at the incomplete-information offer price and sell, in the after-market, at the higher full-information price.[6]

Benveniste and Spindt (1989) show how underpricing and rationing can be used to design a mechanism that ensures truthful revelation. Investors' natural incentive to bid low in the marketing phase entails a trade-off: while it increases the stagging profit, it also jeopardizes the probability and size of their allocations. The carrot that underwriters can offer to regular investors for truthfully revealing pertinent information is a large allocation in underpriced offers, while the stick is the threat to strike them off their distribution lists in future flotations if

---

[6] This assumes that, once trading starts, prices will fully reveal all available information—in other words, that the market is informationally efficient.

Table 3.6. The marketing explanation of IPO underpricing

Result	Source	Empirical evidence	
1 Underwriters can entice 'informed' investors to truthfully reveal their superior information pre-sale; underpricing ensures incentive-compatibility.	Benveniste and Spindt (1989) Sternberg (1989)		
2 Flotations for which positive information is revealed will be priced towards or beyond the upper end of the initial price range; however, the final price will be set below the full-information price to allow regular investors to be compensated via underpricing.	Benveniste and Spindt (1989) Weiss Hanley (1993)	Yes: Weiss Hanley (1993)	[USA]
3 Similarly, the number of shares to be issued is more frequently increased above the initially proposed level, the greater the final offer price in relation to the initial range.	Weiss Hanley (1993)	Yes: Weiss Hanley (1993)	[USA]
4 Underpricing is positively related to the level of interest in the pre-market; in particular, issues eventually priced in the upper part of the offer price range are more underpriced ('partial adjustment phenomenon').	Benveniste and Spindt (1989)	Yes: Weiss Hanley (1993) Sternberg (1989)	[USA] [USA]

Table 3.6. (*cont.*)

Result	Source	Empirical evidence	
5 Underpricing is positively related to the *ex ante* marginal value of investors' private information.	Benveniste and Spindt (1989)		
6 Investment banks give priority to regular investors; doing so minimises underpricing; regular investors will, from time to time, help underwriters by taking up any slack in under-subscribed offers.	Benveniste and Spindt (1989)	Yes: Weiss Hanley (1993) *institutional investors* No: Keloharju (1996) Tinic (1988) *institutional investors*	[USA] · [Finland] [USA]
7 Underpricing is higher in countries with binding restrictions on allocation and/or pricing, than in countries with no such restrictions; it is highest in countries which require both 'even-handed' allocation and non-discriminatory pricing.	Benveniste and Wilhelm (1990)	No: Loughran *et al.* (1994)	[25 countries]

material information is withheld. Since regular investors buy repeatedly from the same underwriter, they thus have underpricing rents to lose from misbehaviour. Note that, while underwriters cannot eliminate underpricing altogether, they can reduce it by using their access to well-informed investors. This contradicts Baron and Holmström's prediction that underwriters' privileged access to information increases underpricing.

Benveniste and Spindt's model seems highly relevant given the current trend towards book-building in Europe, but it may be less useful in explaining the earlier European underpricing experience. Nevertheless, it is worth looking at the cross-sectional evidence. An important testable implication emerging from the model concerns the relationship between the initial price range and the final offer price. A flotation for which positive information is revealed will have a final offer price towards the upper limit of the range, or—if the information is particularly positive—above the range. However, we should not expect this to lead to no underpricing, as some discounting is necessary to compensate informed investors for their truthful revelation. This latter phenomenon is well-documented (cf. Weiss Hanley 1993) and is known as the 'partial adjustment' phenomenon: rather than increasing the final offer price to the full-information price, underwriters adjust the price only partially, allowing investors to gain underpricing returns. Moreover, Benveniste and Spindt point out that IPOs whose final price is close to the initial price ceiling should be more underpriced than those priced in the lower part of the range. The intuition here is that issues for which negative information is revealed do not require regular investors to be compensated via underpricing. Table 3.6 presents the testable implications and the as yet rather limited evidence of the marketing approach.

3.4.2 Pricing and quantity restrictions

While Benveniste and Spindt show that underwriters have an important marketing role to fulfil which may reduce the underpricing discount, in reality their efforts are frequently constrained by regulatory restrictions or institutional conventions. Benveniste and Wilhelm (1990) point out that the marketing process can be constricted in two dimensions:

- most countries impose pricing restrictions to the effect that

underwriters are prohibited from price-discriminating between subscribers;
- quantity restrictions impose a certain allocation rule on underwriters, for instance 'even-handedness' in countries that require *pro rata* allocations or 'wide share ownership' in many privatization programmes.

These restrictions may weaken the underwriters' ability to reduce the winner's curse when some investors are better informed than others.[7]

When price discrimination is possible, there is a fundamental trade-off facing underwriters. On the one hand, by favouring regular, informed investors in allocations, they can reduce the winner's curse and thus the required underpricing among uninformed retail subscribers, at the cost of rewarding regular investors for their truthful revelation of positive information. On the other, underwriters can favour retail customers, which reduces the cost of inducing revelation but aggravates the winner's curse and thus widens the required underpricing discount offered to the uninformed. Though not numerous, there are some countries that allow discretionary quantity and price setting, typically by conducting an auction-type offering to institutional investors and a subsequent retail offering at a different price. Examples include Japan (post 1989), Singapore (post 1992), and Portugal.

Ruling out price discrimination means that underwriters have to offer the same discount to all investors—which is inefficient when only one group needs to be compensated to optimize pricing. This restriction is in force in the USA: the National Association of Securities Dealers' Rules of Fair Practice require uniform pricing. Similarly, ruling out discretionary allocation prevents underwriters from forming valuable long-term relationships with informed investors in the spirit of Benveniste and Spindt's model, implying a sub-optimally and needlessly high level of underpricing. Worse still, ruling out *both* discretionary allocations and price discrimination, underwriters have no means by which to compensate informed investors for providing information, so none will be forthcoming, leading to the full winner's curse and hence lower IPO proceeds.

Internationally, one would thus expect lower underpricing in more 'permissive' capital markets. The institutional framework in the UK, for example, which typically forbids both discretionary allocation and

---

[7] Note that here the *existence* of underpricing is due to asymmetric information and a winner's curse, while institutional factors affect the level/extent of underpricing.

pricing,[8] would hence engender greater underpricing than that in the USA, which merely restricts pricing. Similarly, underpricing in Singapore should have fallen following the liberalization of price and quantity restrictions in 1992—a proposition that remains to be tested. Loughran, Ritter, and Rydqvist (1994) classify 25 countries by the relevant institutional constraints but fail to find any clear support of Benveniste and Wilhelm's prediction, perhaps because of other cross-country differences which they do not control for, such as company size or *ex ante* uncertainty. Disturbingly, however, they claim that uniform pricing tends to be the norm even in countries that have no legal, regulatory or other requirement to that effect.

3.5 Summary

Before turning to more explicitly institutional reasons why firms may wish, or be forced, to underprice their initial public offerings, it is worthwhile to summarize the asymmetric information literature. While we have no doubt that simple averages of underpricing returns, computed across a large number of firms, are unrealistic in ignoring the effects of rationing and perhaps even an informational allocation bias, we do not think that such a winner's curse should necessitate underpricing unless the issuer expressly desired the participation of uninformed investors, a point we will return to in Chapter 7 when discussing governments' objectives in encouraging wider share ownership. Similarly, the notion of initial underpricing as a deliberate signal of quality does not seem convincing—outside, perhaps, the USA—for reasons of logic and institutional differences across countries. Models that build either on marketing and information production or on the principal–agent problem between issuer and investment banker, on the other hand, are appealing in that they afford underwriters an economically valuable role (which is totally absent in both the winner's curse and signalling models) and make what we think are realistic assumptions regarding the underlying distribution of information. However, further tests are needed before a final empirical verdict can be made in this regard.

---

[8] With the recent introduction of book-building techniques in the UK, it has become possible to discriminate between those investors—typically, institutions—who participate in the international tender offers. However, there remains a requirement that shares allocated to public offers be allocated fairly.

4

INSTITUTIONAL EXPLANATIONS

Two main institutional underpricing models will be considered in this chapter. First, the litigiousness of American investors has inspired a *legal insurance hypothesis* of underpricing. The basic idea, which goes back at least to Logue (1973*b*) and Ibbotson (1975), is that companies knowingly sell their stock at a discount to insure against future lawsuits from shareholders disappointed with the performance of their shares. The notion doubtless has some superficial appeal, but for a variety of reasons it is has little economic relevance, as we will argue.

Second, one of the services underwriters provide in many countries is *price stabilization*, a marketing pledge to reduce downward price fluctuations in the after-market. They achieve stabilization via price support, typically by placing a limit order to buy shares as soon as share prices fall below the offer price. Price support is withdrawn after a certain period of time, as specified by regulators, the underwriting contract, or market conditions. In Chapter 7, we will discuss the various forms that price stabilization can take in the context of privatizations. Here, we will focus on its implications for underpricing.

The most obvious institutional explanation of underpricing, and one that we shall not pursue further here, is political interference. No doubt there are many countries, not only in the developing world, which have seen their political elites enrich themselves and their cronies via favourable allocations of deeply discounted IPOs. Similarly, some markets impose regulatory constraints on the price formation process which almost automatically lead to high discounts, such as the requirement that companies be floated at no higher than a particular price earnings ratio. But meddlesome politicians and archaic valuation methods cannot explain the very existence of underpricing: something else must account for the discount at which, say, US or European companies are floated.

4.1 Legal Liability

Stringent disclosure rules in the USA expose underwriters, account-
ants, and issuers to considerable litigation risk: shareholders can sue
them on the grounds that material facts were mis-stated or omitted
from an IPO prospectus. Securities class action lawsuits are notoriously frequent in the USA: in 1986, for instance, Alex. Brown & Sons
and L.F. Rothschild, Unterberg, Towbin, two major-bracket investment banks, were involved in more than 130 separate IPO lawsuits
between them.[1]

Tinic (1988) and Hughes and Thakor (1992) argue that intentional
underpricing may act as insurance against such securities litigation.
Lawsuits are obviously costly to the defendants, not only directly—
legal fees, diversion of management time, etc.—but also in terms of the
potential damage to their reputation capital: litigation-prone investment banks may lose the confidence of their regular investors, while
issuers may face a higher cost of capital in future capital issues. Hughes
and Thakor postulate a trade-off between minimizing the probability
of litigation and hence minimizing these costs on the one hand, and
maximizing flotation revenue (and the underwriters' commission
thereon) on the other. Crucially, they assume that the former increases
in the offer price: the more overpriced an issue, the more likely is a
future lawsuit. In addition, underpricing reduces not only (i) the probability of a lawsuit, but also (ii) the probability of an adverse ruling
conditional on a lawsuit being filed, and (iii) the amount of damages
awarded in the event of an adverse ruling (since actual damages in the
USA are limited by the offer price). Some further testable implications
regarding underwriters' reputation are listed in Table 4.1.

The tightening of disclosure and liability requirements in the 1933
Securities Act provides a convenient regime shift along which to test the
hypothesis. Prior to the 1933 legislation, the principle of *caveat emptor*
applied to the securities industry in an almost unfettered way, so firms
and banks faced virtually no litigation risk. Since 1933, on the other
hand, underpricing should have risen in line with the increased risk of
future litigation. Tinic's results, reported in Table 4.1, seemingly confirm this, although her samples (70 flotations from 1923 to 1930, 134
new issues from 1966 to 1971) may be too limited and unrepresen-

---

[1] The figures are quoted in Tinic (1988).

tative, given our knowledge of the immense variability in average underpricing over time. Moreover, New Zealand, which according to Vos and Cheung (1992) has a similar legal environment to the USA, saw no change in underpricing following its introduction of tough liability legislation in the 1983 Securities Regulations Act, a regime shift similar to the enactment of the 1933 Securities Act in the USA. While Tinic does find support for those of her conjectures that are derived from underwriter reputation, her conjectures are sufficiently general to be consistent with just about any underpricing explanation. For instance, lower underpricing among more reputable banks is equally consistent with a reduced winner's curse or superior information production during the marketing phase.

More light can be shed on the issue by investigating the effect of underpricing on the probability of litigation.[2] The most thorough evidence is due to Drake and Vetsuypens (1993), who among other things document that underpricing does not reduce the probability of a lawsuit: purchasers of underpriced offerings are just as likely to sue in the USA as purchasers of overpriced ones, and firms that are sued are no more or less underpriced than comparable companies that are not sued. In our view, these observations seriously undermine the lawsuit avoidance hypothesis, despite the undeniable identification problem of not being able to rule out the existence of firms that did manage to escape lawsuits by virtue of underpricing.

Whatever the empirical success, or otherwise, of the lawsuit avoidance theory, the legal literature has voiced profound scepticism. Alexander (1993) contends that the hypothesis is based on misleading or overly simplistic assumptions about actual legal and financial liability for underwriters and issuers: (i) underwriters do not in reality bear the costs of litigation and thus have no incentive to insure themselves; moreover, the greatest part in any settlement is paid by insurance companies under directors' and officers' liability policies and not by parties to the IPO agreement; (ii) underpricing would offer only limited protection because it is irrelevant in suits brought under the 1934 Securities Exchange Act, which in practice is virtually always invoked alongside the 1933 Securities Act; and (iii) since the Acts are about disclosure and not pricing, a finding of underpricing is

---

[2] Since most cases are settled out of court, settlement and legal costs are difficult to assess and the impact of underpricing on the probability of an adverse ruling and on the amount of damages are hard to analyse in the USA.

Table 4.1. The lawsuit avoidance explanation of IPO underpricing

Result	Source	Empirical evidence
1 In order to avoid legal liability for mis-statements in the IPO prospectus, underwriters and issuers rationally choose to underprice IPOs.	Logue (1973a) Ibbotson (1975) Tinic (1988) Hughes and Thakor (1992)	Yes: Tinic (1988) [USA] No: Drake and Vetsuypens (1993) [USA] Lee et al. (1994) [Australia] Keloharju (1993b) [Finland] Ljungqvist (1995a) [Germany] Beller et al. (1992) [Japan] Vos and Cheung (1992) [NZ] Rydqvist (1994) [Sweden] Kunz and Aggarwal (1994) [Switzerland] Jenkinson (1990) [UK]
2 Underpricing reduces the probability of litigation.	Tinic (1988)	No: Drake and Vetsuypens (1993) [USA]
3 Underpricing reduces the conditional probability of an adverse judgment if litigation occurs.	Tinic (1988)	
4 Underpricing reduces the amount of damages in the event of an adverse judgment.	Tinic (1988)	
5 Lawsuit avoidance should not have mattered before the 1933 Securities Act, so underpricing should be lower before 1933.	Tinic (1988)	Yes: Tinic (1988) [USA]

6	Underpricing is smaller, the more experienced the underwriter is at due-diligence investigations.	Tinic (1988)	Yes: Tinic (1988)	[USA]
7	The greater is *ex ante* uncertainty, the higher is expected underpricing.	Tinic (1988) Hughes and Thakor (1992)	See Table 3.2.	
8	Underwriters with large-reputation capital at stake avoid speculative small IPOs.	Tinic (1988) Hughes and Thakor (1992)	Yes: Tinic (1988)	[USA]
9	Underpricing is lower, the better the underwriter's reputation.	Hughes and Thakor (1992)	Yes: Tinic (1988) Carter and Manaster (1990)	[USA] [USA]
10	When there are unusually many speculative IPOs ('hot issue' periods), the market share of fringe underwriters should increase.	Tinic (1988)	Yes: Tinic (1988)	[USA]
11	Owing to liability being joint-and-several, issuers that refuse to use underpricing as legal insurance have to compensate underwriters via larger spreads.	Tinic (1988)		
12	If underwriters' compensation and the equilibrium probability of litigation increase in the IPO price, then underpricing is larger, the lower the compensation.	Hughes and Thakor (1992)		
13	On average, underpricing is higher if no underwriter is used.	Hughes and Thakor (1992)	Yes: Muscarella and Vetsuypens (1989*a*)	[USA]

immaterial to the outcome of litigation. She concludes that underpricing would be an inefficient and ineffective means of obtaining insurance against securities law violations.

The lawsuit idea is a good example of a US-centric model which fails in the international context: underpricing is a global phenomenon, while strict liability laws are not. The risk of being sued is not economically significant in Australia (Lee, Taylor, and Walter 1994), Finland (Keloharju 1993b), Germany (Ljungqvist 1995a), Japan (Beller, Terai, and Levine 1992, Macey and Kanda 1990), Sweden (Rydqvist 1994), Switzerland (Kunz and Aggarwal 1994), or the UK (Jenkinson 1990), all of which experience underpricing. A more promising institutional approach is price support, to which we turn next.

4.2 Price Support

Rather than forming a symmetric distribution around some positive mean, underpricing returns typically peak sharply at zero, are highly positively skewed, and include few negative observations. Ruud (1991, 1993) takes this statistical regularity as her starting point to argue that underwriters do *not* underprice deliberately—rather, they price IPOs at expected market value and support those offerings whose prices fall below the offer price in after-market trading. Such behaviour will tend to eliminate the left tail of the cross-sectional initial return distribution, and thus lead to the observation of a positive average price jump. According to Ruud, what we perceive is not the unconditional expectation of true initial returns—which she argues might very well be zero—but the expectation *conditional* upon underwriter intervention: if price support suppresses the negative tail of the initial return distribution, companies merely *appear* to be underpriced on average. Ruud (1993) estimates the unobserved unconditional mean of the return distribution in a Tobit model and indeed finds first-day returns close to zero, as her price support hypothesis would suggest.

There is further evidence of potential intervention. For a sample of 72 large IPOs, Schultz and Zaman (1994) report that on average US underwriters repurchase a stunning 21 per cent of the original number of shares on offer during the first three trading days, while Asquith, Jones, and Kieschnick (1995) find that about half of all US IPOs in 1982–1983 must have been supported. This strongly suggests that underwriter intervention in support of after-market prices is both large-scale and widespread, at least in the USA. If provided temporarily, price support is legal in many countries, including the USA (1934 Securities Act, Rule 10b-7), the UK (Securities and Investments Board Rules, Chapter III, Part 10), France (Husson and Jacquillat 1989), Germany (Ljungqvist 1995*a*), Greece (Panagos and Papachristou 1993), Hong Kong (McGuinness 1993*b*) and the Netherlands (Jansen and Tourani Rad 1995).

4.2.1 *The value of price support*

Investors clearly value stabilizing activities, for they put a floor under early after-market prices and act as insurance. Moreover, price support may reduce the winner's curse experienced by uninformed investors, which may be of particular importance in privatizations. Analytically, we can think of price support as a put option written by the underwriter and held by the initial subscribers. Not unlike underpricing, the put option could thus be seen as part of the compensation that underwriters offer investors for their information production, as in Benveniste and Spindt (1989).

Typically, banks cannot be legally held to the price support promises they make during the marketing phase, but perhaps the repeat nature of underwriting activities ensures that they do not renege, *ex post*, on their pledge. Unless they hedge their price support,[3] banks stand to lose quite considerable amounts, not only in terms of the opportunity cost of tying up capital in acquiring IPO shares, but also in terms of the possibility of later having to dump the acquired shares at a loss. It is thus not certain why underwriters should willingly engage in stabilization efforts: how are they compensated for offering investors the put option? Ruud (1993) and Weiss Hanley, Kumar, and Seguin (1993) make only vague allusions to reputational effects from which an underwriter might benefit over time. The simplest form compensation could take—higher underwriting spreads—remains untested.

Schultz and Zaman (1994) suggest the following compensation mechanism. In the USA, investors have the right to renege, without legal sanction, on their 'indications of interest' or even firm IPO orders for five trading days. Given the fact that the 10–15 per cent caps imposed on underwriting spreads by many US states frequently bind, banks cannot pass the cost of providing such a 'cooling off' put option

---

[3] The use of over-allotment options for these purposes will be discussed in Chapter 7.

on to the issuers. Instead, they may try to lower the probability of investors exercising their put options, by promising price support which limits investors' downside risk, and by setting a lower strike (IPO) price—that is, by underpricing. This line of reasoning combines price stabilization with the more traditional view of deliberate underpricing, viewing the two as complements rather than substitutes. The typical empirical finding that positive returns tend to persist for more than a month of trading after which, presumably, price support should have been withdrawn, is consistent with Schultz and Zaman's view that price support alone cannot explain away positive initial returns.

Benveniste, Busaba, and Wilhelm (1995) offer a different explanation of why underwriters provide price support, by formalizing Smith's (1986) informal notion of stabilization as a bonding mechanism. As we discussed in the previous chapter, the fact that commission increases with gross flotation proceeds gives underwriters an incentive to set a higher offer price. They could, for instance, overstate investor interest during the marketing phase in order to start a cascade. Clever IPO investors will recognize this adverse incentive and, in the absence of any counteracting force, will not bid for shares. By committing themselves to price support—which is costlier, the more the offer price exceeds 'true' share value—underwriters are seen to be keeping the temptation to overprice in check, which, if believed, will ensure continued investor participation in the IPO market. However, perfect precommitment is unlikely to be possible, unless investors can enforce pledges of price support made during marketing. This, Benveniste *et al.* argue, will lead to greater deliberate underpricing than if credible commitment were possible.

4.2.2 Price support and underpricing: substitutes or complements?

There are thus three distinct views as to what explains underpricing. The observed price jumps can be due to (i) price support alone, as Ruud argues, (ii) underpricing alone, as much of the rest of the literature suggests, or (iii) price support in conjunction with old-fashioned underpricing, as Schultz and Zaman and Benveniste *et al.* argue. We can illustrate the substitutes *v.* complements debate using Rock's (1986) winner's curse model. If investors are hedged against downside risk some or most of the time, why should there be any need to underprice in compensation for uninformed investors' winner's curse?

Asquith, Jones, and Kieschnick (1995) try to discriminate between the three schools of thought by means of a statistical analysis of the return distributions. First, they note that not all IPOs will be supported and, therefore, there will be two distinct distributions: one for supported offerings and one for unsupported ones. What one observes in any sample of new issues is the mixture of these two distributions. If Ruud is correct in saying that there is no deliberate underpricing, then the initial return distribution of unsupported offerings should have a mean of zero. This, however, is not what Asquith *et al.* find. Instead, unsupported firms are underpriced by about 18 per cent, while supported ones are not underpriced once the effects of price support in eliminating the left tail of that distribution are taken into account. Thus, the authors favour explanation (iii): underpricing and price support are complements rather than substitutes, and any theoretical explanation that relies only on one of these will be misleading.

4.2.3 Testable implications and evidence

The lack of publicly available information with which to distinguish supported from unsupported IPOs gives rise to testing by proxy.[4] The most commonly adopted procedure is to view overpriced, fully priced, and sometimes even modestly underpriced issues as likely support candidates, but one should note the imperfect nature of this approach. Two other unknowns are the time length of stabilization and the time pattern of the intensity of intervention. The power of empirical tests then depends on whether anything can be said *a priori* about the effects that price support should have on observable variables. In other words, the testable implications are key.

   Schultz and Zaman use detailed transactions data for a small sample of US IPOs and find support for the various market microstructure implications that follow from price support (summarized in Table 4.2). In particular, for new issues that start trading close to the offer price, underwriters quote higher bid prices and are vastly more likely to be on the buy side rather than the sell side, compared with other market-makers. The innovation in Weiss Hanley, Kumar, and Seguin's (1993) model is to view price support as insurance aimed primarily at rival market-makers, rather than initial investors. As the evidence

   [4] In October 1983, the US Securities and Exchange Commission ceased to require filing of reports in respect of any price supporting bid. In a regrettable act of data destruction, the SEC subsequently destroyed all records of which new issues had received price support until 1983, making it impossible to identify supported IPOs in the USA (cf. Ruud 1993).

Table 4.2. The price support explanation of IPO underpricing

Result	Source	Empirical evidence
1 Underwriters stabilize after-market trading prices at the offer price, thus minimizing the occurrence of overpricing; price support provides investors with a put option, written by underwriters.	Ruud (1991, 1993)	Yes: Ruud (1991, 1993) [USA] *Initial returns are non-normal and peak at zero; almost no negative tail.*
2 In addition to the explanation of underpricing in 1, underwriters underprice to lower the implicit strike price and thus the value of the put option to investors.	Schultz and Zaman (1994)	
3 Through price support, underwriters provide other dealers with a put option; this reduces market makers' costs and thus leads to narrower spreads.	Weiss Hanley *et al.* (1993)	Yes: Weiss Hanley *et al.* (1993) [USA] Miller and Reilly (1987) [USA]
4 Underwriters spend more time at the highest bid for cold IPOs (IPOs trading at or below their offer price) than for hot IPOs.	Schultz and Zaman (1994)	Yes: Schultz and Zaman (1994) [USA]
5 For cold IPOs, underwriters spend more time at the bid than at the ask.	Schultz and Zaman (1994)	Yes: Schultz and Zaman (1994) [USA]
6 Underwriters spend more time at the bid than at	Schultz and Zaman (1994)	Yes: Schultz and Zaman (1994) [USA]

the ask compared to other market-makers, especially for cold IPOs.

7	Underwriters quote higher bid prices than other market-makers, especially for cold IPOs.	Schultz and Zaman (1994)	Yes: Schultz and Zaman (1994) [USA]
8	As a percentage of total volume, sell volume is greater for fully priced than for underpriced IPOs.	Schultz and Zaman (1994)	Yes: Schultz and Zaman (1994) [USA]
9	Price support lowers the volatility of after-market returns.	Panagos and Papachristou (1993)	No: Panagos and Papachristou (1993) [Greece]
10	Higher-quality underwriters are more likely to engage in price support.	Ruud (1991, 1993)	Yes: Ruud (1991, 1993) [USA]
11	Over time, underwriters remove price support.	Ruud (1991, 1993) Weiss Hanley et al. (1993)	Yes: Ruud (1991) [USA] *Prices of fully-priced or just-underpriced IPOs more likely to fall than to rise over first four trading weeks.* Weiss Hanley et al. (1993) [USA] *Spreads widen and prices fall over time.* Schultz and Zaman (1994) [USA] *Underwriters permanently reduce the supply of cold-IPO shares.*
12	*Ceteris paribus*, the larger the syndicate, the greater its resources, the more likely it is to support prices; the larger the offering, the more likely the syndicate to underprice instead.	Chowdhry and Nanda (forthcoming)	

confirms, the price guarantee seems to lower market-makers' liquidity risk and accordingly leads them to charge lower bid–ask spreads, consistent with their downside risk being capped by the lead-managers' price-stabilizing limit order. As intervention ceases, prices for support candidates seem to fall while bid–ask spreads widen, although Schultz and Zaman show that, rather than banks trickling the acquired shares back into the market, intervention permanently reduces the supply of IPO shares.

To summarize, underwriters certainly have opportunity, and may have a motive, to intervene in secondary market trading. There is abundant circumstantial evidence that such intervention has real effects on the trading behaviour of IPOs. What seems less credible is that price support alone can account for the empirical underpricing regularity, as Ruud initially postulated. More likely, stabilization is either a complement to underpricing or helps to mitigate it. We will return to its effects in Chapter 6, where we discuss the long-run performance of new issues.

5

OWNERSHIP AND CONTROL

....

Going public is, in many cases, a step towards the separation of ownership and control which is so characteristic of common law economies.
The owner–manager who raises funds for investment from outside
investors, the founder family that sells out to a new management team,
or the firm that floats a minority stake in a subsidiary—all change the
company's ownership structure in a flotation. Ownership matters for
the effects it can have on the management's incentives to make optimal
operating and investment decisions. In particular, where the separation
of ownership and control is incomplete, an agency problem (Jensen
and Meckling 1976) between non-managing and managing shareholders arises: rather than maximizing expected shareholder value,
managers may maximize the expected private utility of their control
benefits (say, perquisite consumption) at the expense of outsiders. The
existence of such agency costs has long been recognized. However, they
would appear to be particularly pertinent to small firms going public
and raising large amounts of money, as opposed to the more usual
scenario of rights issues by large already-listed companies whose
managers hold only tiny equity stakes.

There are two principal models which have sought to rationalize the
underpricing phenomenon within the bounds of an agency cost approach. Their predictions are diametrically opposed: while Brennan
and Franks (1995) view underpricing as a means to entrench managerial control and the attendant agency costs by *avoiding* monitoring
by a large outside shareholder, Stoughton and Zechner's (1995) analysis instead suggests that underpricing may be used to minimize agency
costs by *encouraging* monitoring.

In this chapter, we will develop these two models in greater detail. In
our view, this literature is interesting for the different interpretation
it offers of underpricing. Similar to the undoing of Modigliani and

Miller's (1958) famous capital structure irrelevance proposition, the choice of a particular level of underpricing will here affect the future cash flows of the firm and thus its value, implying that underpricing per se is not a valid measure of the efficiency of the flotation process. However, the literature is as yet relatively speculative and the empirical verdict is still out.

5.1 Underpricing as a Means to Retain Control

Brennan and Franks (1995) develop a model in which underpricing gives managers the opportunity to protect their private control benefits by allocating the issue strategically when taking their company public. Managers would wish to avoid any large stakes being assembled by a single investor for fear that their non-value-maximizing behaviour would receive unwelcome scrutiny. By deliberately underpricing the flotation, they can ensure that the offer is over-subscribed and thus that investors will need to be rationed in their allocations. Rationing, in turn, allows managers to discriminate between applicants of different sizes and so to reduce the block size of new shareholdings. With smaller new stakes there will be less monitoring, owing to two free-rider problems. First, because it is a public good, shareholders will invest in a suboptimally low level of monitoring (Shleifer and Vishny 1986). Second, greater ownership dispersion similarly implies that incumbent managers benefit from a reduction in the threat of being ousted in a hostile takeover (Grossman and Hart 1980), giving them an added incentive to engineer a diffuse shareholder structure. Vigilant non-managing shareholders or outside directors might be expected to exercise managerial discretion in keeping the flotation price in check, but at least in the USA IPO firms have proportionately fewer outside directors than listed companies, while a majority (55 per cent) of the equity is held by management prior to going public (cf. Beatty and Zajac's 1995 survey of the 1984 IPO cohort). In Japan also, IPO firms are unusually tightly controlled by directors, with unusually low institutional shareholdings (cf. Cai and Wei 1996).

5.1.1 Testable implications and evidence

The two principal testable implications to emerge from the Brennan–Franks model concern the relationship between underpricing on the

Table 5.1. Ownership and control explanations of IPO underpricing

Result	Source	Empirical evidence
1 IPOs are deliberately underpriced to create, via over-subscription and rationing, a more *dispersed* ownership structure. This . . .		
1a . . . creates a free-rider problem which will minimize the possibility of challenges to the manager–shareholders' ('directors') control of the firm and thus protect the private benefits they enjoy at the expense of non-directors;	Brennan and Franks (1995)	
1b . . . provides a more liquid secondary market for the shares;	Booth and Chua (1996)	
1c . . . creates a free-rider problem which helps controlling owners to extract more surplus from a potential after-market buyer of the rest of the firm.	Zingales (1995)	
2 In order to protect their private benefits, directors use underpricing and the consequent over-subscription to discriminate against large applications and in favour of small ones.	Brennan and Franks (1995)	Yes: Brennan and Franks (1995) [UK] SEC (1971) [USA]

Table 5.1. (*cont.*)

Result	Source	Empirical evidence
3 If rationing implies more diffuse shareholdings post-IPO, then it is more costly to assemble large stakes in the after-market; therefore, the higher underpricing, the smaller the blocks assembled after the IPO.	Brennan and Franks (1995)	Yes: Brennan and Franks (1995) [UK]
4 Directors should not sell many shares, so their share of underpricing costs should be lower than non-directors'.	Brennan and Franks (1995)	
5 The lower the fraction of underpricing costs borne by directors, the greater are their incentives to use underpricing to protect their private benefits, so the greater is underpricing.	Brennan and Franks (1995)	Yes: Brennan and Franks (1995) [UK]
6 IPOs are deliberately underpriced to create a more *concentrated* ownership structure; this ensures that managerial discretion is mitigated by monitoring through a large external shareholder.	Stoughton and Zechner (1995)	

one hand and the initial size and subsequent secondary market evolution of equity blocks on the other (cf. Table 5.1). Using detailed proprietary data on individual applications and allocations in 13 UK flotations, Brennan and Franks confirm that large applications are discriminated against in favour of small ones, an effect that is stronger the more an issue is underpriced and oversubscribed.[1] The US Securities and Exchange Commission, in its 1971 Institutional Investor Study Report, similarly reported that underwriters typically divide oversubscribed issues into very small allocations.

The obvious objection to Brennan and Franks's reasoning is that the effect of discriminatory allocations could easily be undone: shareholders receiving smaller-than-desired allocations could simply re-adjust their stakes in the secondary market. Brennan and Franks counter this objection by asserting that such open-market purchases may not be profitable. If the market anticipates the gains that would accrue if management were monitored by a sufficiently large outside shareholder, prices will rise in response to large-scale buying. This will tend to make it unprofitable to assemble a large block of shares in the after-market, the more so the more diffuse the ownership structure is to start with. In other words, the marginal cost of assembling large stakes in the secondary market must increase in the initial ownership dispersion at flotation for underpricing to be useful in entrenching management. If this is true, one would expect smaller blocks to be assembled after IPOs with greater underpricing. Using a larger sample of 43 new issues, Brennan and Franks confirm this prediction.

A somewhat unintuitive corollary of Brennan and Franks's model is the assumption that, for purely exogenous reasons, the non-managing shareholders are keen to liquidate part of their stakes. This ensures that the flotation can go ahead in the first place: otherwise the rational response of non-directors to managers' flotation plans would be to avoid selling underpriced shares at the IPO and instead to sell out in the secondary market. The exogenous liquidity constraint that Brennan and Franks impose amounts to non-directors being held hostage by managers: either they surrender the pricing decision to the managers, or the company won't go public. Whether this is a reasonable

---

[1] The need for detailed data unfortunately limits Brennan and Franks's sample size: post-flotation ownership information is available for 43 firms, pre-IPO ownership data for 28, and allocation data for 13. The 69 IPOs Brennan and Franks identify overall for 1986–1989 represent less than 14 per cent of all firms coming to market in that period, which raises some doubt as to the representativeness of the results.

assumption is best judged against the empirical evidence. Brennan and Franks show that non-directors sell as little as possible at the IPO (subject to the constraint of floating at least 25 per cent as required by the London Stock Exchange), while directors sell only a tiny fraction of their stakes at flotation. Moreover, over the following seven years, non-directors' holdings are almost entirely eliminated, while directors sell very little. This is consistent with non-directors evidently wanting to sell out but minimizing the underpricing cost.

Finally, the Brennan–Franks model predicts that underpricing is greater, the lower the fraction of underpricing costs borne by directors, since this increases their incentives to use underpricing to protect their private benefits. The evidence here is more mixed. It is true that directors, as predicted, sell fewer shares than non-directors and thus empirically suffer only half the underpricing costs that non-directors bear. But this may simply be due to managers owning smaller stakes—and thus having fewer shares to sell—than non-managing shareholders before flotation.

5.1.2 Discussion

By and large, the evidence is *consistent* with Brennan and Franks's model. However, intent is very difficult to infer from any of it: directors may sell few shares at flotation, hold on to most of their holdings in the following few years, and be content with large applications being discriminated against, for reasons other than entrenchment. In particular, two rival models offer quite different interpretations of the value of greater ownership dispersion. Booth and Chua (1996) argue that owners do underprice, as in Brennan–Franks, in order to achieve a more dispersed ownership structure via over-subscription and rationing. But their motive for doing so is, innocently enough, to provide a more liquid secondary market for their shares. Zingales (1995), on the other hand, argues that firms seek a diffuse ownership structure in order to extract more surplus from a potential after-market buyer of the shares. Greater dispersion creates a free-rider effect not dissimilar to the one preventing outside shareholders from profitably assembling large after-market stakes in Brennan–Franks. Consistent with this, Pagano, Panetta, and Zingales (1995) document that most Italian flotations are followed by private transfers of ownership and control from the original founders to new owners. Other evidence is sparse. Brennan and Franks do not disclose how many of their sample firms changed hands post-flotation. Goergen (1995) finds a relatively large incidence of control changes in German IPO firms but does not specifically test Zingales's model.

The available evidence so far does not allow us to discriminate between the Brennan–Franks, Booth–Chua, and Zingales models. Since these models go well beyond trying to explain why we observe underpricing, the key to distinguishing them is not to do with underpricing, but with the more fundamental question why firms go public in the first place. In Brennan and Franks's model, firms are floated for exogenous reasons (non-managers wish to liquidate their stakes), while Booth and Chua and Zingales base the going public rationale on the potential benefits of a public listing (greater trading liquidity or efficient transfers of control).

Whatever the empirical success of the Brennan–Franks model, there are at least two good reasons to doubt its practical relevance. First, if British managers are so worried about greater scrutiny, why don't they issue non-voting stock? The London Stock Exchange does not formally prohibit issuance of non-voting shares, which surely would be the best way to retain control of the company and all attendant private benefits. Similarly, in countries where non-voting stock is regularly issued, Brennan and Franks would predict no underpricing, as the control retention argument fails. However, many German and Swedish companies have floated only non-voting shares but have been underpriced, on average, by just as much as firms selling voting equity— which indicates that underpricing has causes independent of mere control considerations. Moreover, if discriminating against potential monitors is so important in the UK, why not move to a system that optimizes discrimination? Book-building gives issuers wide-ranging discretion to discriminate against any investors on the basis of their identity. This is a much more refined way of fine-tuning the post-flotation ownership structure than the crude rationing strategy based on application size. Book-building is certainly quickly becoming the offering method of choice in continental Europe, and has been used in recent privatization offerings and other large international flotations in the UK (Wellcome's being a good example). But, far from eliminating the need to underprice, book-buildings still appear to be floated at the typical 10–15 per cent IPO discount!

5.2 Underpricing as a Means to Reduce Agency Costs

At the heart of the Brennan–Franks approach is the assertion that, in the wake of the separation of ownership and control, managers try to maximize their expected private utility by entrenching their control benefits. However, there is a hidden assumption underlying this belief which deserves discussion. Granting that managers' incentives are likely not to be perfectly aligned with owners' interests in many firms on the threshold of a public listing, directors may actually wish to allocate the issue in a way that minimizes—rather than maximizes— the scope for managerial discretion. Why? Agency costs are ultimately borne by the owners of a company, in the form of a lower flotation and subsequent market value for their shares. To the extent that managers are part-owners, they bear some of the costs of their own non-profit-maximizing behaviour. If their stakes are large enough that the agency costs they bear outweigh the private benefits they enjoy, it will be in their interest to reduce, not entrench, their discretion. The post-flotation ownership structure may therefore increase firm value by affecting the efficiency of corporate governance.[2] Brennan and Franks must implicitly assume that this trade-off is, in practice, decided in favour of entrenchment.

Based on this intuition, Stoughton and Zechner (1995) observe that, in contrast to Brennan and Franks, it may be value-enhancing to allocate shares to a large outside investor who is able to monitor managerial actions. Monitoring, as we have already noted, is a public good. Since any large shareholder will monitor only in so far as this is privately optimal (which is a function of the size of her stake), there will be under-investment in monitoring from the point of view of both shareholders and incumbent managers. To encourage better monitoring, managers may try to allocate preferentially a particularly large stake to an investor. However, if the allocation is sub-optimally large from the investor's point of view, an added incentive may be offered in the form of underpricing. Such underpricing may not even represent an opportunity cost: in the absence of monitoring, the firm would have had to be floated at a lower price anyway, owing to outside shareholders anticipating the extent of managerial agency costs.

---

 [2] Cf. Burkart, Gromb, and Panunzi (1995) for a formal analysis of the trade-off between too little monitoring (managerial discretion) and too much monitoring (intrusive interference in managerial initiatives).

A closer look at Stoughton and Zechner's model is constructive. The selling mechanism is modelled as a two-stage process akin to book-building. In the first stage, issuers extract the demand schedule from a likely monitor and set the offer price such that this investor optimally chooses a large enough number of shares to engage subsequently in effective monitoring. In the second stage, small investors are allocated shares at the same price (unless price discrimination is possible, which in practice it rarely is). Rationing is observed at this stage as small investors would like to buy further shares at the low offer price. The set-up is reminiscent of Benveniste and Spindt's (1989), but here under-pricing is not a measure of the efficiency of the selling mechanism. The Benveniste–Spindt argument turns on the value of the information that can be extracted from institutional investors during the marketing phase and which allows firms to obtain a keener price in a two-stage sale than they would in an auction. In Stoughton and Zechner's model, on the other hand, underpricing is higher in a two-stage sale than in a Walrasian auction (where it would be zero), but that is beside the point: the auction would not allow the issuer to treat large investors favourably and thus reap the value-enhancing benefit of monitoring—which more than offsets the underpricing cost.

As in the marketing literature we reviewed in Chapter 3, owners would prefer a discriminatory allocation and pricing regime which would allow them to favour a potential monitor but would not extend the underpricing discount to small investors. Consequently, allocational freedom would lead to the optimal use of underpricing. Empirically, we would expect a three-point underpricing regulation scale as follows: countries that prohibit price and/or quantity discrimination should experience higher underpricing, on average, than countries with lightly-regulated offering mechanisms, which in turn will have higher discounts than countries that have compulsory auctions. This prediction is the same as Benveniste and Wilhelm's (cf. Chapter 3), but again the international evidence, reported in Loughran, Ritter, and Rydqvist (1994), is inconclusive: there is no clear empirical relationship between a country's offering mechanism and the level of underpricing it experiences.

This concludes our overview of underpricing theories and evidence. We will return to these matters in Chapter 8, where we will offer our assessment of the theoretical literature as well as some suggestions on optimal pricing. In the meantime, we will turn our attention to theoretical explanations for the long-run underperformance phenomenon.

6

LONG-RUN PERFORMANCE

....

The most recently discovered stylized fact, the tendency of new issues to underperform in the long-run, is the least-well understood regularity in the IPO literature. Is it an equilibrium phenomenon that arises from some asymmetry in information endowments or from institutional peculiarities? Or are we faced with evidence of irrational behaviour by the investing public? Or is it instead simply a figment of our imagination, the result of our inability to measure long-run performance precisely, to control for risk correctly, and to devise statistical significance tests properly?

At this point, a definitive answer still eludes us. The explanations that have been offered remain speculative in nature, owing to the relative lack of structured tests designed not merely to produce results consistent with some theory or other, but rather to falsify their testable predictions. The three sections of this chapter will explore the above questions in turn, reviewing the existing conjectures, contributing new hypotheses, and assessing the available evidence.

The first section concentrates on the question whether long-run underperformance has any place in the underpricing models discussed in the preceding three chapters. Few studies have attempted to explain both underpricing and long-term underperformance in a unified framework. In some cases, long-run performance results can shed light on the plausibility of an explanation for underpricing, as in the signalling approach whose long-term predictions meet with little empirical support. While the literature has not yet begun to explore the links between the two phenomena, at least one promising avenue for future research emerges here in the guise of price support. The second section is devoted to expectations-based and behavioural explanations of long-run underperformance, while the final section addresses the problems of return and risk measurement over extended event windows.

6.1 Long-Run Underperformance in Theories of Underpricing

6.1.1 Signalling

Of the asymmetric-information-based underpricing models surveyed in Chapter 3, only signalling and marketing have anything to say about long-run performance. Rather than predicting that newly floated companies will underperform in the long run, signalling theories seem to require *positive* after-market returns, given that firms underprice in order subsequently to be able to sell further shares at a higher price than in the absence of the signal. A falling share price would hardly be consistent with the strategy of multiple-stage sales assumed in the signalling approach: why delay divestment if IPO firms on average perform poorly? A rather obvious empirical corollary is hence that only firms experiencing positive share price performance should return to the equity market within a short period of time.[1] This indeed seems to be the case in the USA, the UK, and Germany.

Of course, long-run performance studies typically measure performance relative to some benchmark. Thus, the poor abnormal returns we documented in Chapter 2 do not necessarily rule out that absolute share prices at the time of any subsequent equity sales are higher than initial trading prices. However, it is easy to control for this, simply by looking at both raw and excess returns. The average German IPO firm, for instance, traded below its first-day price after three years (after adjusting for stock splits, etc.) and managed a raw three-year return of 5 per cent only as a result of dividend payments (cf. Ljungqvist 1996c).

For the average IPO firm, therefore, signalling seems to make no sense. However, what is true on average may not be true across the quality distribution of issuers. In particular, if firms underprice to signal, and if a separating equilibrium obtains in this game, high-quality

---

[1] This is assuming that the sole reason why firms sell seasoned equity is because they planned to do so when they devised their signalling strategy for flotation. Of course, there are plenty of other reasons for equity issues which will add noise to empirical testing.

firms should—perhaps by virtue of this signal—perform better than low-quality ones. A number of testable implications emerge. Assuming that companies do follow the underprice-to-signal strategy, (i) firms issuing seasoned equity should be high-quality (this is implied by successful separation); (ii) they should hence outperform non-reissuing firms, in terms of both share price performance (as discussed above) and operating performance; (iii) firms that underprice should exhibit superior post-listing performance relative to those that do not; (iv) in order to reap the benefits from signalling, any seasoned equity issue should be undertaken as soon as is possible lest the signal is dissipated; and (v) firms that float smaller equity stakes (in anticipation of later seasoned offers), which on the reckoning of the signalling models means high-quality firms, should outperform those retaining relatively small stakes.

The first prediction is hard to test, as any definition of what constitutes a high-quality issuer is inherently subjective. We are not aware of any direct attempts at making such a definition operational. The second prediction finds support at least as far as share price performance is concerned (cf. Table 6.1), although operating performance—as yet unstudied in the present context—would probably make for a more clear-cut test. Prediction (iii) is soundly rejected in every country where it has been studied: greater underpricing and better long-run performance—be it share price (cf. Ritter 1991) or operating (cf. Jain and Kini 1994) performance—do not go hand-in-hand. The evidence we discussed in Chapter 3 does not indicate that firms return to the market sufficiently quickly for the underpricing signal not to be dominated by other information, violating prediction (iv). Finally, while the last prediction does receive some support in Singapore, it is contradicted by the German evidence.

In our view, the poor empirical performance of these predictions provides the final nail in the coffin of the signalling models. In Chapter 3, we discussed a number of reasons why we doubt their practical relevance, notably the fact that the underpricing signal may well be dominated, in cost-effectiveness terms, by the certification role performed by reputable investment bankers and other professionals. Here, we have argued that the long-run performance results are inconsistent with what are, in our opinion, logical implications of signalling, leading us to conclude that signalling retains little credibility as an explanation of underpricing.

Table 6.1. Equilibrium explanations of IPO long-run performance

Hypothesis	Source	Empirical Evidence	
Signalling			
1 Firms raising further equity financing after their IPO are high-value and hence outperform non-issuing firms.	—	Yes: Levis (1993b) Michaely and Shaw (1994) Ljungqvist (1996a)	[UK] [USA] [Germany]
2 Firms that underprice exhibit superior post-listing returns relative to those that do not.	—	No: Jain and Kini (1994) Ritter (1991) Ljungqvist (1996a) Cai and Wei (1996)	[USA] [USA] [Germany] [Japan]
3 The greater their quality, the more capital firms retain initially and the better they perform; thus, expected long-run returns increase in the retention rate.	—	Yes: Koh et al. (1992) No: Ljungqvist (1996a)	[Singapore] [Germany]
Marketing			
4 Companies priced at the upper end of the initial price range should perform better than those priced at the lower end.	Weiss Hanley (1993)	No: Weiss Hanley (1993)	[USA]
Legal liability			
5 The finding of underperformance is due to failure to include value of legal damages in performance evaluation.	Hughes and Thakor (1992)	No: Alexander (1993)	[USA]

Price support

6 The long-term underperformance finding may be due to price support; if so, firms whose shares where initially supported should underperform if measured from the first trading day,…	Ljungqvist (1996c)	Yes: Ljungqvist (1996c)	[Germany]
7 …but should perform neutrally if measured from the date when support is withdrawn.	Ljungqvist (1996c)	Yes: Ljungqvist (1996c)	[Germany]
8 (*corollary*) Firms not receiving price support should perform neutrally when measured from the 1st trading day.	Ljungqvist (1996c)	No: Ljungqvist (1996c)	[Germany]

Agency costs

9 The less managers' equity stakes are reduced at flotation, the better the long-run operating performance will be.	—	Yes: Mikkelson and Shah (1994)	[USA]
10 The greater managerial equity stakes post-flotation, the better the long-run operating performance will be.	—	Yes: Jain and Kini (1994)	[USA]
		No: Mikkelson and Shah (1994)	[USA]
		Cai and Wei (1996)	[Japan]

6.1.2 Marketing

Benveniste and Spindt's (1989) model of underpricing as a marketing tool is pertinent also to our understanding of long-run performance. If a final offer price in the upper part of the initial range indicates that investors revealed positive information about the firm and its prospects, we would expect such firms to perform better in the long-run than companies whose final price was set towards the lower part of the range. This provides a cross-sectional implication which is easily testable in the USA and other countries which use marketing mechanisms similar to book-building. Furthermore, it may even explain the existence of underperformance: if there are more cases of negative information than of positive information, long-run performance may well be negative on average. However, the only available evidence to date is unsupportive: firms priced above the initial range in Weiss Hanley's (1993) US sample did not fare any better than those priced below it.

6.1.3 Legal liability

Hughes and Thakor (1992) argue that their legal insurance model of underpricing is consistent with long-run underperformance, if along with the underwriter the issuer also is liable for damages. They interpret damages as extra 'dividends' paid out by the firm to its shareholders. IPO investors are effectively buying a package consisting of a share and a 'litigation put' which enables them to recover part of any subsequent losses from the issuer. Failing to include the monetary value of these 'litigation dividends' in calculations of long-run returns, the authors argue, will result in an understatement of true economic returns and may lead to the observation of spurious underperformance.

However, we do not concur with this view, partly for the reasons noted in Chapter 4, and partly because, as legal scholars such as Alexander (1993) have pointed out, 'litigation dividends' would in practice not be available during the first three or five years of trading, the period over which underperformance is usually observed. The fact that litigation risk is not economically significant in many countries, such as most European and many Asian markets, which nevertheless experience underperformance, leads us to conclude that legal reasons can probably not explain the poor after-market returns earned by IPO firms.

6.1.4 Price support

The practice of price support, however, may well be consistent with both underpricing and poor long-term returns. If first-day trading prices are kept artificially high by supportive underwriters, they are the wrong starting point for a long-run performance evaluation. Once support is withdrawn, prices will adjust downwards to the true market equilibrium. Starting the clock on the first trading day thus wrongly leads to an observation of negative returns. If many IPOs receive such price support, it is conceivable that the resulting estimation bias is sufficiently large to lead to a spurious finding of abnormal underperformance.

Three testable implications emerge: (i) offerings whose initial prices were supported should have poor long-run abnormal returns if measured from the start of trading, but (ii) not compared with the end of the support period; (iii) conversely, issues not initially supported should perform neutrally on average.

The principal difficulty in testing these predictions is one of identification: which new issues were initially supported, and at what time was support withdrawn? In the absence of such information, any test must rely on—invariably inferior—proxies. Ljungqvist (1996c) proposes two ways to address the problem. First, he argues that overpriced and fully priced IPOs are more likely to have been supported than underpriced ones. He therefore compares the long-run performance of overpriced issues with that of the cohort of *ex post* underpriced offerings, but fails to find any empirical support for the price support hypothesis: underpriced offerings perform no better or worse than overpriced ones.

Second, he follows the approach that Ruud (1991, 1993) advocated to identify the existence of price support in a market. Looking at the price behaviour of those issues that started trading at, or slightly above, their offer prices, Ruud found that over the following four weeks the great majority of these saw prices drop—an experience not shared by IPOs in general. She conjectures that the drop is due to the withdrawal of price support. If so, those offerings that experience this pattern would be expected to perform poorly in the long run if performance is measured from day 1, but not if it is measured from the end of the support period, say the third or fourth trading week. Ljungqvist's inconclusive evidence on this score—while predictions (i) and (ii) are supported, (iii) is not—may be due to the imprecise nature of the identification procedure. In our view, further work in this area is warranted.

6.1.5 *Agency costs: separation of ownership and control*

The operating performance literature has proposed an explanation for poor long-term performance based on Jensen and Meckling's (1976) conflict of interest between managers and shareholders. With the reduction in managerial ownership as a firm sells shares to a wide(r) circle of investors may come an increase in agency costs: managers' incentives to maximize firm value rather than private benefits (say, perquisite consumption) decrease in the fraction of equity capital held by outside shareholders. Consequently, firm performance will suffer post-flotation—unless the relative size of the managers' stakes is unaffected by the transition to public ownership, as would be the case if the firm sold only either the non-managerial portion of a capital increase or secondary shares held by non-managing shareholders.

This idea can easily be put to a test. If issues in which the relative size of managers' equity stakes remains unaltered at flotation do not experience poor long-run operating performance, while firms whose managers' equity stakes are reduced at flotation do, agency costs may well explain declining operating performance. In addition to this change effect, there may be a levels effect: the greater the managerial equity stakes post-flotation, the better a company performs in the long run. We will discuss the evidence in a moment. We note first, however, that Jensen and Meckling's divergence-of-interests hypothesis has been challenged outside the IPO literature. DeAngelo and Rice (1983) and Stulz (1988) argue that high levels of managerial ownership concentration will limit the effect of the market for corporate control in disciplining non-profit-maximizing managers, precluding the possibility of hostile takeover. This entrenchment effect may lead managers to pursue private benefits at the expense of outside minority shareholders. Whether the entrenchment or divergence-of-interests effect dominates depends on the level of managerial ownership, a prediction supported empirically in Morck, Shleifer, and Vishny (1988).

At first glance, the IPO evidence seems mildly supportive of the existence of a divergence of interests. Mikkelson and Shah (1994) find a positive relationship between operating performance and the change in the fraction of equity capital held by officers and directors in the USA: the more managers' stakes decline at flotation, the worse is post-listing operating performance. Curiously, while the authors concede that this correlation is consistent with the Jensen–Meckling explanation, they are reluctant to attribute it to it. As to the levels effect, the evidence is more mixed. Jain and Kini (1994), who do not discriminate between managers' and non-managers' relative participation in the public offering, find a positive relationship between post-flotation operating performance and overall retention rates, as predicted in the presence of Jensen–Meckling agency costs. Using a more comprehensive sample which partly overlaps with Jain and Kini's data, however, Mikkelson and Shah instead find a negative relationship between the same variables. For Japanese issuers, there is no relationship between changes in profitability and managerial ownership.

Moreover, Loughran and Ritter's (1994) study of seasoned equity offerings throws doubt on divergence-of-interests as the primary determinant of poor operating performance: many already-listed firms are widely held when seasoned equity issues are initiated, but they experience the same pattern of anomalous declines in operating performance post-issue as do IPO firms. Given that a seasoned equity issue should not change the agency cost status quo much, this would argue against a conflict-of-interest explanation.

However applicable the agency cost argument may be to the observed decline in operating performance following equity issues, it is a questionable explanation of long-run share-price underperformance. Rational IPO investors should take changes in managers' incentives into account when valuing newly listed firms. In other words, worsening agency problems should not come as a surprise and thus should not be reflected in poor returns. Hence, increased agency costs cannot explain, in a semi-strongly efficient market, what happens to share prices.

6.1.6 Discussion

No underpricing theory predicted, before Ritter's seminal (1991) paper, that IPOs would underperform in the first few years after flotation. *Ex post* attempts at arguing that long-run underperformance is in fact consistent with this or that underpricing model have not, as we have argued, proved particularly fruitful. The one approach that we believe holds promise is price support. However, much more—and better!—evidence is needed before the practical merits of this idea become clear. In the meantime, we turn next to behavioural explanations of anomalous long-run performance.

6.2 Behavioural Explanations of Long-Run Underperformance

6.2.1 Heterogeneous expectations

E. M. Miller (1977) explores the effect on asset pricing of relaxing the usual assumption of homogeneous expectations. Allowing investors to have different opinions about the future cash flows and growth potential of an enterprise introduces an element of realism which perhaps can help explain long-run underperformance. A crucial feature of the model is that, given the small size of the typical flotation, a small number of investors is usually sufficient to absorb the entire outstanding stock of a firm. If there is divergence of opinion, this minority will consist of those punters who are most optimistic about the company in question. Rather than reflecting the unbiased evaluation of all publicly available information, as the efficient markets hypothesis would require, the market-clearing share price under heterogeneous expectations will be set by the marginal investor who is just optimistic enough about the prospects of a company to buy its shares. This may account for the initial price jump: first-day buyers are particularly optimistic about the firm, and buy even though it is widely known that no further underpricing gains can be hoped for beyond the opening trade. The very fact that there are investors who are willing to buy from staggers during the first few days, and thus hand these subscribers tidy underpricing profits, suggests there must be a fair amount of optimism around.

As the divergence in opinion becomes smaller, the marginal investor's evaluation and hence the trading price are lowered. If—as seems likely—heterogeneity is greatest at flotation but declines over time with the arrival of more information, the fact that a handful of once optimistic investors lower their appraisal of a company will drive the price down, even though the *average* assessment might never have changed. It is worth pointing out that the new information need not even be particularly negative; any piece of information that decreases the spread of opinion about a firm will lead to a lower price.

Applying Miller's model to long-run performance, two empirical implications arise. First, long-run performance should be negatively related to the initial extent of divergence of opinion, a prediction which is in practice hard to test—how to measure divergence of opinion? One possible answer is to use initial trading volatility and volume as proxies:

the more volatile and the more heavily traded a flotation, the greater the initial spread of expectations. However, we know of no existing tests along these lines. Second, long-run performance should be negatively related to the speed with which heterogeneity is reduced by new information: long-run returns decline sooner, the faster expectations converge. Again, the difficulty of measuring the extent of heterogeneity and the speed of adjustment has, so far, precluded empirical testing.

One possible theoretical objection to Miller's model is that, logically, there should be one pessimistic investor for every optimistic one, who via short-selling would put downward pressure on share prices such that firms are priced at (roughly) expected value. More precisely, since a market with many overoptimistic investors but a small number of arbitrageurs and a fully rational, homogeneous market are observationally equivalent, there must be some structural or institutional reason why arbitrageurs cannot take advantage of the predictable trading patterns of Miller's model. The obvious such reason is the practical difficulty of implementing an IPO shorting strategy: casual empiricism, reported in Loughran and Ritter (1995), suggests that shorting new issues is hard even in a well-developed market such as the American one, at least in the first few months of trading. More seriously, perhaps, the accumulated evidence of poor IPO performance should sooner or later put pressure on the divergence of opinion—surely, even optimistic investors must eventually draw the conclusion that new issues are not worthy of such high expectations. Whether this learning process will, in the future, lead to the disappearance of the long-run performance anomaly remains to be seen. Meanwhile, Miller's model can potentially explain both initial underpricing and subsequent underperformance.

6.2.2 Fads and timing

It is only a small step from Miller's model to the claim that primary-market investors behave irrationally. Aggarwal and Rivoli (1990), for instance, argue that there are fads in the IPO market, with investors initially being over-optimistic about the prospects of newly listed companies and bidding up initial trading prices beyond fair value. This assertion goes to the heart of traditional underpricing models, which assume that the immediate after-market values a flotation efficiently. According to Aggarwal and Rivoli, one cannot rule out the possibility that it is the—lower—long run rather than the initial trading price that reflects a firm's true value. This would imply that the notion of IPO underpricing is a misnomer: the first-day price jump is due not to the offer price having been set too low, but rather to faddish investors over-valuing a firm when trading starts. However, this raises two questions: (i) why don't investors learn from past mistakes? and (ii) why don't issuers take full advantage of investors' over-optimism by raising offer prices until there is no longer a price jump?

There is some evidence which may indicate that investors indeed consistently overestimate the future prospects of firms coming to market. Mikkelson and Shah (1994) show that long-run share price performance and the change in operating performance from before to after flotation are negatively related: when operating performance fails to sustain pre-listing levels of profitability, share prices fall, indicating that investors were surprised by the change in operating performance. Jain and Kini (1994) document that at flotation investors value IPO companies at unusually high price–earnings and market–book ratios (compared with matched non-issuers), but that these decline signifi-cantly over time in line with the fall in operating performance. What this proves is unclear, however. Given recent evidence on the cross-section of expected returns (cf. Fama and French 1992), we note that the market–book ratio may proxy for non-beta risk factors as well as investors' expectations of future earnings growth.

Loughran, Ritter, and Rydqvist (1994) go one step further than Aggarwal and Rivoli. Noting a curious coincidence of years in which many firms go public and the buoyancy of the equity market, they assert that companies may be able to predict when over-optimism is most likely to occur. If so, firms will time their flotations to coincide with these windows of opportunity during which particularly favour-able offer prices can be obtained. As more information becomes available, investors correct their initial overvaluation, leading to poor long-run returns.

This, of course, is a much stronger claim than the mere existence of fads. Loughran et al.'s explanation rests on the—rather tenuous—assumption that companies are somehow able to tell a temporary fad, which will soon revert to normality, from a sustainable rise in valuations. Even if it is true—which is far from clear—that investors consistently and mistakenly extrapolate past earnings growth when valuing newly listed firms and thus overpay, crediting companies with the ability to predict time variations in investor sentiment seems highly unrealistic.

The empirical evidence, listed in Table 6.2, is mixed. Ali (1995) investigates whether the market's estimates of the prospects of IPO firms are optimistically biased. Comparing the 'optimistic bias' in analysts' consensus earnings forecasts for issuers and matched non-issuers, he finds that, while analysts tend to be unduly optimistic in general, they are more over-optimistic about issuers than about non-issuers. Moreover, this bias is greatest for smaller issuers which Ritter (1991) and Loughran and Ritter (1995) show underperformed particularly badly. Cheng (1996) shows that US companies which are expected not to use the proceeds of seasoned equity issues for investment purposes underperform more than investing firms, a finding that is consistent with the non-investing firms selling equity because they are overvalued (cf. Myers and Majluf 1984). The fact that both types of issuers significantly underperform the market is troubling, though: granted that the non-investing firms underperform solely because they 'timed' their issue, why do the investing firms also underperform?

On the other hand, Leleux (1992) finds a negative relationship in the USA between the extent of initial underpricing and the time to distressed delisting, which he argues is inconsistent with investor overreaction: if investors did initially overpay as a result of over-optimism, underpricing should be unrelated to fundamental firm value, and therefore should not affect attrition rates. The fact that firms that are relatively more underpriced are delisted sooner than less underpriced ones instead suggests that underpricing leaves firms undercapitalized.[2] For seasoned offerings, managers have no incentive to 'market time' in countries with pre-emptive rights, as no wealth transfers from new to existing shareholders are involved. Nevertheless, South Africa—where this is the case—has a similar degree of long-run underperformance to the USA (see Affleck-Graves and Page 1995). Looking at the effect of various proxies for investor sentiment on long-run performance, Ljungqvist (1996a) fails to find any evidence of companies' supposed timing ability in Germany. And finally, I. Lee (1994) shows that directors' and other insiders' trading in the USA is unrelated to performance subsequent to seasoned equity issues, which strongly suggests that, despite their presumably superior information, managers share the market's mistaken expectations of future cash flows.

---

[2] Incidentally, Leleux's results throw yet more doubt on signalling explanations of underpricing: to the extent that it is high-value firms that signal, they should survive for longer, which is not the case empirically.

Table 6.2. Behavioural explanations of IPO long-run performance

Result	Source	Empirical Evidence
Heterogeneous expectations		
1 Share prices are set by the marginal, most optimistic investor; as information flows increase with seasoning, divergence of expectations decreases and thus prices are adjusted downwards; long-run performance is negatively related to the initial extent of divergence of opinion.	Miller (1977)	
2 Long-run returns decline sooner, the faster expectations converge.	Ljungqvist (1995a)	
Fads and timing		
3 Firms go public when investors are over-optimistic about the growth prospects of IPO companies; investors overpay initially but mark prices down as more information becomes available; expected long-run returns therefore decrease in initial investor sentiment.	Loughran et al. (1994) Loughran and Ritter (1995) Ritter (1991) Rajan and Servaes (1994)	Yes: Rajan and Servaes (1994) [USA] Loughran and Ritter (1995) [USA] Jain and Kini (1994) [USA] Teoh et al. (1994) [USA] Mikkelson and Shah (1994) [USA] Ali (1995) [USA] Cheng (1996) *seasoned issues* [USA]

4 The greater the fraction of equity capital initial owners retain at flotation, the lower their incentive to take advantage of overoptimistic investors since the value of their retained shares would fall as and when the new investors become less optimistic; therefore, expected long-run returns increase in the retention rate.	Ljungqvist (1996a)	No: Högholm and Rydqvist (forthcoming)	[Sweden]
		Ljungqvist (1996a)	[Germany]
		Leleux (1992)	[USA]
		Yes: Koh et al. (1992)	[Singapore]
		No: Ljungqvist (1996a)	[Germany]

6.2.3 Window-dressing

A final link in the behavioural chain is firms' incentives to actively encourage optimistic views of future performance. The US literature has shown that companies typically go public after what appears to be particularly strong operating performance, but then fail to sustain the growth rates achieved in the year or two before flotation. While it is possible that the original owners float their companies after periods of genuinely strong performance, which they—unlike investors—know cannot be sustained in future, it is equally likely that pre-issue performance is a deception.

DeGeorge and Zeckhauser (1993) point out that managers have extraordinary incentives to make their firms 'shine' before flotation. To use their example, consider a manager who owns 10 per cent of a firm which normally earns US$1 million and which will sell at eight times earnings when it goes public. Every US$1,000 increase in pre-flotation earnings means another US$800 for the manager. Compare this with typical performance-related pay increases—Jensen and Murphy (1990) report that a US$1,000 increase in firm value raises median CEO remuneration by a mere US$26—and it is not surprising that managers endeavour to present the best possible figures in their prospectuses.

There are several ways in which managers can engage in 'window-dressing'. First, they can 'borrow' earnings from other periods. To borrow from the future, simply lower prices temporarily to boost sales now, or defer any spending (R&D, staff training) whose returns will occur only in the longer term. Similarly, past performance can be borrowed by slowing down earnings growth in the year before the flotation year. The effect will be stellar performance just before the IPO, with a later decline in operating performance. Of course, investors will expect this and will therefore downgrade the multiple they are willing to pay. Earnings manipulation and the subsequent post-IPO operating performance downturn should not come as a surprise and so should have no share price effect. This is, of course, not true empirically of IPOs.[3]

---

[3] However, DeGeorge and Zeckhauser find it to be true for US leveraged buy-outs (LBOs) which are subsequently refloated: they have the same operating performance pattern as IPOs but perform neutrally compared with matched firms in terms of share price. Reverse-LBOs are different from IPOs in that, having been traded before, more information is available about them at re-flotation; they are similar to large IPOs in terms of size. Ritter (1991) finds that only small IPOs underperform in the long run, so the neutral performance of reverse-LBOs is not inconsistent with IPO long-run performance.

Second, US generally accepted accounting principles (GAAP) give IPO firms great freedom to massage their earnings before initial or seasoned equity issues, including the authority to restate *retroactively* all financial information presented in prospectuses, mainly through the use of accruals. There is evidence, reported in Teoh, Wong, and Rao (1993), that IPO firms make extensive use of this freedom. Finally, managers could fraudulently overstate their earnings performance, an option that may seem a distinct possibility in some less regulated markets around the world, but which empirically plays only a minor role in the USA (cf. Teoh, Welch, and Wong 1995).

While earnings management explains the poor post-issue operating performance, rational investors should not be fooled, and consequently the share price performance should be unaffected by discretionary accounting practices. However, we know this is not the case. In fact, Teoh, Wong, and Rao (1994) and Teoh, Welch, and Wong (1995) show that earnings management and long-run excess returns are significantly negatively related in initial and seasoned offerings. This may suggest that investors are fooled by such discretionary accruals adjustments and initially fail to fully discount them. Having over-estimated future cash flows at flotation, investors mark down share prices when the expected high level of profitability fails to materialize. Mikkelson and Shah's (1994) findings, discussed earlier, paint a similar picture.

In summary, these patterns are consistent with managers playing to investors' over-optimism by 'massaging' accounting ratios to create the impression of superior pre-flotation performance ('window-dressing'), and investors failing to figure such behaviour into initial trading prices. Again, however, the crucial question arises: why don't investors learn? Until a convincing structural or institutional answer is forthcoming, we find it hard to believe that behavioural explanations can solve the new issue puzzle.

6.3 Measurement Problems

Underperformance could have more trivial causes. It might simply be due to bad luck, or to a failure to control properly for risk, or to problems relating to measuring returns over long horizons. Welch (1996) points out that the companies driving Ritter's (1991) results were small, infrequently traded, and bunched in certain specific industries (most notably, oil and gas exploration in 1980) which subsequently

Table 6.3. Mis-measurement explanations of IPO long-run performance

Result	Source	Empirical evidence	
Risk mis-measurement			
1 Long-run under-performance may be due to a failure to adjust returns for time-varying systematic risk; e.g., if betas decline with seasoning time and markets generally fall during the evaluation period, the assumption of constant, unit betas will induce spurious underperformance.	—	No: Ritter (1991) Keloharju (1993*b*) Ljungqvist (1995*a*)	[USA] [Finland] [Germany]

experienced industry-specific exogenous shocks (for instance, the oil price collapse in the early 1980s). Can we therefore rule out the alternative explanation that long-run underperformance merely is due to bad luck? Perhaps not, but the overwhelming evidence from around the world suggests that IPOs are indeed poor long-term bets.

Then there is the possibility that the usual simplifying assumption of unit, time-invariant beta systematic risk for all newly listed firms can seriously bias long-run performance estimation. If, as seems likely, IPOs typically have greater-than-average market risk, at least initially, then wrongly constraining betas to be one will lead to a spurious finding of underperformance when the market index falls over the holding period. Of course, the converse is also true: falsely assuming unit betas in a rising market will impart an upward bias in performance estimates if true betas are greater than one. Which way the bias will go in practice depends on the empirical question of whether IPOs trade mostly in rising or declining markets. Since Clarkson and Thompson (1990) document non-stationary betas for IPO firms in the USA, risk mis-measurement may well account for part—if not all—of the observed underperformance. However, those authors (listed in Table 6.3) who have tried to adjust for beta risk still find that newly listed firms underperform.

Finally, there is a growing literature investigating the statistical power of long-run return metrics, exemplified by Barber and Lyon (1995) and Kothari and Warner (1995). Most of these papers suggest that traditional long-run performance studies based on cumulating abnormal returns produce biased and inefficient results (principally, owing to the positive skewness of the abnormal returns), and thus caution against putting too much store by the underperformance evidence. On the other hand, not every long-run study listed in Table 2.2 above used these inferior techniques and still found underperformance. On balance, therefore, we believe there is still a case to answer.

Part III

POLICY IMPLICATIONS

7

PRIVATIZATION

Privatizations constitute a particular class of initial public offerings, where the vendor is not an entrepreneur (or private investor) but rather the government. In practice, therefore, the main beneficiary of a privatization is usually the Treasury, rather than the company itself, although privatizations are often accompanied by financial restructurings of the companies concerned. In selling previously publicly owned companies, governments essentially undertake a debt–equity swap: raising money from the sale of the equity to private investors in order to reduce the accumulated debt of the public sector. The general public should, as a result, enjoy lower taxes in the future, although collectively they no longer have any claim on the assets sold. In this conventional model, any discount on the IPO constitutes forgone future general tax reductions, with all the benefits accruing to those investors who successfully applied for shares at the IPO. An alternative model, which has been widely used in Eastern Europe and elsewhere, is simply to give the company away to all citizens in the form of free shares. In this way equality of treatment is assured, although the government raises no funds as a result of the transfer into private ownership.

In terms of revenue raised by IPOs, privatizations have dominated the new issue market in many countries in recent years. This has been particularly true in the UK: Jenkinson and Trundle (1990) report that over the period 1985–1990 £23.6 billion was raised via IPOs, of which £16.7 billion was raised by government privatizations. Figure 7.1 charts the total proceeds from UK privatizations (including revenue raised via IPOs but also secondary equity offerings and trade sales), and shows the enormous scale of the programme. In the period 1980–1995, over £61 billion has been raised by the government.

However, while the UK may have been an early pioneer of privatization, its popularity has spread widely in recent years; this can be seen

Fig. 7.1. Proceeds from UK privatizations

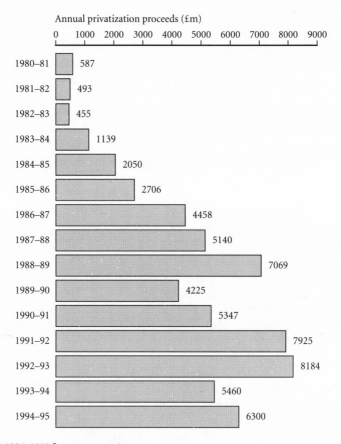

Note: 1994–1995 figures are an estimate.
Source: H.M. Treasury (1995)

in Table 7.1, where the expected privatization proceeds for the period 1993–1995 are presented for a number of European countries.

Privatizations raise many additional concerns that we consider in this chapter. Governments often attempt to achieve multiple objectives via privatization, such as the extension of private share ownership. Such objectives can result in the government actually aiming to under-price the shares in privatized companies, viewing the forgone revenue as the price of achieving such objectives.

Table 7.1. Privatizations in Europe, 1993–1995

	Proceeds ($bn)		
	1993	1994	1995
Austria	0.6	1.5	1.9
Belgium	1.1	1.5	0.5
Denmark	0.2	5.7	0.3
Finland	0.2	0.9	0.2
France	8.1	10.7	9.9
Germany	0.5	1.1	4.7
Greece	0.0	0.2	0.0
Italy	2.3	9.0	6.5
Netherlands	0.8	3.9	1.7
Norway	0.2	0.2	0.2
Portugal	0.5	1.1	1.9
Spain	3.0	3.2	2.3
Sweden	0.8	3.4	2.0
UK	8.0	8.5	8.5
Total Europe	25.8	50.8	40.5

Source: NatWest Securities, quoted in *Financial Market Trends*, OECD, February 1995.

We look critically at such arguments in the next section. In Section 7.2 we consider the various techniques available to governments conducting a privatization programme. In the final section of this chapter we show how the various objectives and available techniques interact, illustrating the discussion with reference to the extensive UK privatization programme, and draw some general policy conclusions.

7.1 Privatization Objectives

There are some important ways in which privatization IPOs may differ from those conducted by private-sector companies. Governments often use privatizations to achieve multiple, often conflicting, objectives, some of which are concerned with broad public policy issues that are of no interest to private-sector firms going public. We explore below the impact of these various objectives on the way privatization IPOs have been structured. However, although in this chapter we concentrate on the issues relevant to the way privatizations are conducted, it is worth noting that the most important objective that most governments aim to achieve through privatization is simply to promote the efficiency of the companies concerned.

In this section we first examine the objectives before considering in the next section the various available techniques that are used in privatization IPOs.

Objective 1: revenue raising

Revenue raising is the most obvious objective of many privatizations. Governments are able to use privatization proceeds to reduce public borrowing, which may result in reduced taxation in the future. However, it should be noted that governments also lose a claim on the net cash flow generated by the companies sold, and so taxes will be lower in the future only if the sale proceeds exceed the net present value of the future earnings that would have been earned under public ownership. In practice, it will be difficult to know whether this condition is satisfied, although in many cases the net cash raised for the public purse from privatization (taking account of balance sheet restructurings before the sale) have been quite limited. Clearly, the value of any firm that is sold will reflect investors' expectations of *future* profitability, taking account of any anticipated efficiency savings resulting from the transfer into private ownership. What is noticeable in the case of many privatizations is that, unlike private-sector IPOs, the longer-term performance of the companies has often been extremely strong, suggesting that at the time of the IPO investors were not aware of the extent of the inefficiencies existing under public ownership. This suggests that, quite apart from the more technical considerations about how privatization IPOs should be conducted, government should attempt to rationalize and improve efficiency as much as possible before the sale of the company, in order to appropriate as many of the gains as possible for taxpayers rather than the initial shareholders. A further implication may be that some form of 'clawback' of unanticipated profits should be considered, although such provisions will inevitably depress the initial sale price. (However, this effect will be outweighed in the event of such unanticipated profits materializing.)[1] An alternative approach, which we consider more fully below, is the use of staged sales, so that the government retains an equity interest in the future performance of the company.

As has been argued earlier in this book, discounts on IPOs are essentially transfers between the original owners of the company and those that are allocated shares at the IPO. In the case of a privatized company the initial owner is the government, and the wealth transfer that takes place in the event of the IPO being discounted is between taxpayers in general and the initial shareholders. These wealth transfers will often be *ad hoc*, depending on who participates in the privatization IPO and who is allocated shares in the event of over-subscription, and will frequently be regressive, with wealthier members of society participating to a greater extent that those with few financial resources to invest in the IPO. As a consequence, one aim of governments should be to maximize the proceeds of the flotation, although governments differ considerably in the vigour with which they pursue this objective.

Objective 2: wide share ownership

Privatizations have been used by many governments to encourage participation in the stock market by individual investors. It is not entirely clear, however, why this should be a public policy objective. The UK government state explicitly that 'the promotion of wider and deeper share ownership—both among employees and the general public—is part of the Government's policy of extending the ownership of wealth more widely in the economy, giving people a direct stake in the success of British industry, and removing the old distinctions between "owners" and "workers" ' (H.M. Treasury 1995, p. 4). Of course, all taxpayers had a stake in British nationalized industries anyway, albeit indirectly, and to the cynic therefore the privatization programme can only lead to a consolidation of the ownership of wealth, rather than to an extension of it. Some have argued (see, e.g., Jenkinson and Mayer

---

[1] An example of such provisions is the claw-back of profits from future property development that may be carried out by Railtrack, the UK railway track operator. Railtrack has been privatized with a large portfolio of land of unknown commercial value. The government has therefore made an assumption as to how much Railtrack will make out of the exploitation of these assets, and any amount up to the assumed sum will be retained by shareholders. Any excess will be shared between shareholders and customers (via reductions in track access charges).

1988) that if wide share ownership is a public policy aim it could be more efficiently achieved via the provision of tax breaks to equity ownership; for example, a certain amount of dividend income and capital gain arising from equity investment each year could be tax free.

The latter objective of encouraging workers to have a stake in their companies clearly has much more substance, and may contribute significantly to increased efficiency. However, it is worth noting that standard portfolio theory would suggest that such individuals, who already have significant amounts of human capital invested in the company they work for, should actually diversify their equity port-folios to include companies other than the one they work for in order to reduce risk. While the encouragement of employee share ownership may have excellent incentive effects, it may none the less encourage an inefficient allocation of investment funds.

Many countries include wide share ownership as a key objective of privatization but few have pursued the objective as vigorously, or for as long, as the UK. Evidence from the UK suggests, however, that, after over 15 years of privatization, share ownership, while wider, is not deeper, and that few additional investors have regularly bought non-privatization shares. For example, the number of small shareholders in 1979 numbered around 3 million, rising to around 11 million in 1991 before falling back to just over 9 million in 1993. However, according to the partly government-funded Pro-Share, which tracks share owner-ship, 72 per cent of all retail investors hold shares in only one or two companies. The clear evidence is that many of the early privatizations, which were discounted very heavily, simply induced stagging by retail investors. For example, the British Aerospace privatization in 1981 attracted 26,000 retail investors, although soon after the sale the number of small investors had fallen to just 3,000. More recently, the privatization of the 12 regional electricity companies in 1991 resulted in 35 per cent of retail investors selling their shares within the first month of trading.

Moreover, from the theoretical perspective the wide share owner-ship objective can create problems. Many of those potential investors who are the target of government attempts to broaden the shareholder base will often be relatively uninformed, certainly in comparison with institutional investors. The existence of investors with diverse infor-mation will inevitably result in winner's curse problems, with the result that discounts will have to increase in order that uninformed investors earn a reasonable rate of return. Hence attempts to broaden share ownership are likely to be directly in conflict with the realisation of revenues that are close to asset valuations.

It is possible that some of these problems can be avoided, or at least reduced, by giving preferential allocations to individual investors in the event of excess demand for the privatization shares. Many recent privatizations have used multi-part offerings with a book-building exercise aimed at institutional shareholders operating alongside a domestic public offer, for example. Governments often employ a 'claw-back' technique whereby if the public offer is over-subscribed then less stock is allocated to institutional investors. This biasing of allocations in the event of excess demand should certainly help to increase the expected returns to the relatively uninformed investors, although it will not remove the negative returns that may occur if an issue is under-subscribed.

Objective 3: government credibility

Whatever the weight given to the various objectives of government in privatizing—and these vary greatly across countries—there is a fundamental difference between privatizations and IPOs conducted by private-sector companies. Unlike private companies, for whom an IPO is a one-off event, governments typically own a whole range of assets which can be sold off sequentially as part of a privatization *programme*. As a result, individual privatizations cannot be viewed in isolation: a government may, quite rationally, want to invest in a reputation (for instance, for selling companies at fair prices) during the early phases of a privatization programme, to encourage investor participation in later stages. There have been many examples of government privatization programmes being set back significantly by an overpriced issue, or by a company that performs poorly in the after-market. For example, the Spanish privatization programme started running into difficulties in 1995 following the poor performance of previous privatization offerings (e.g. Argentaria's share price had fallen by around 35 per cent since its sale in November 1993). In order to reverse negative investor sentiment, it was necessary for the Spanish government to re-stimulate interest in the privatization programme, and it chose, in addition to discounting the shares in the next sale—Repsol—to offer investors a one-year money back guarantee, which would compensate investors for any losses up to 10 per cent. (We discuss such schemes more fully below.) The important lesson is that investors can quickly become disillusioned with privatizations and that the cost to a government, especially one in the early stages of an extensive privatization programme, of losing credibility may be considerable, and may be difficult to reverse. Consequently, governments rightly place importance on privatizations being viewed as a 'success', although, as will be discussed more fully later in this chapter, there are various ways of promoting the participation of investors that are more sophisticated than simply underpricing the shares by an enormous amount.

The importance of government reputation may also influence the *structure* of privatizations. As Guney and Perroti (1993) point out, even after a firm is privatized, it may still be vulnerable to changes in government policy. The most obvious examples of these problems relate to industries that are still regulated by government after privatization, such as many utility industries. In these cases there may be advantages to the use of staged sales, whereby the government retains a stake in the company for some period of time. The retention of an equity interest should reduce the temptation to change policy in a way that would reduce the value of the firm, and should therefore increase the confidence of potential investors in the credibility of government policy.

Objective 4: effective control

One of the main arguments for privatization is that control is shifted from the public sector to private capital markets. Companies are required to report in a standard format to investors on a regular basis and are subject to the analysis and criticism of investors and analysts. However, there are two concerns that arise regarding the effectiveness of the corporate control mechanism for privatized companies.

First, wide share ownership may have detrimental control implications. A large number of very small shareholders may provide little effective monitoring of management, principally due to free-rider and co-ordination problems. However, in practice, institutional investors soon come to dominate the share registers of most privatized companies, so this argument should not be over-stated.

Second, in many cases governments retain a special share in the company that bestows certain control rights. Examples include the 'golden shares' existing in many UK privatized companies (see Table 7.3 below for details) and the *noyeaux durs*—or 'hard nuts'—owned by the French government. These special shares are put in place for various reasons—for example to protect certain industries deemed to be of strategic importance from foreign takeover—but their effect is inevitably to weaken the corporate control exercised by the capital market. In many cases such shares may remove entirely the threat of a hostile takeover, which in some countries is likely to be far more potent as a threat than the direct intervention of investors. However, some special shares are of limited time duration, and in some cases governments have waived their control rights when a change in corporate control has been proposed (for example in the case of Ford's takeover of Jaguar). It should also be remembered that governments rarely allow the capital market a completely free hand in corporate control, as competition and industrial policy (whether exercised at the national or supranational level) will frequently constrain potential mergers and changes in ownership.

7.2 Privatization Techniques

7.2.1 Methods of Sale

Public offers Most privatization issues contain a public offer of the shares. The form that public offers take differs considerably across countries, but most are aimed directly at involving small shareholders, with some also embracing larger institutional shareholders. Many early privatizations, such as the early UK offers, were conducted entirely through public offers, with no segmentation of the offer into different components aimed at institutional and/or foreign investors. The advantage of public offers is that they can be used to promote wide share ownership as all members of the public are invited to participate in the offer. However, there are a number of drawbacks with privatizations conducted solely through a public offer.

First, pricing the issue can be extremely difficult. There may be relatively little information available to the government or its advisers as to the likely demand for the shares and hence the appropriate issue price. Some of the most spectacular examples of underpricing have resulted from privatization public offers, and as a result there has been a tendency towards the use of techniques that allow information about demand to be gathered before the price is set, rather than simply setting the price and waiting to see the extent of demand.

Second, in many countries the price in a public offer has to be set some considerable time (typically five to ten days) before the shares are allocated, so that investors have time to receive the final prospectus and submit their bids. Such a time delay exposes the issue to much uncertainty, not least regarding movements in the stock market as a whole between the date the price is set and the final date for applications. A particularly graphic example of such problems was the sale of the second tranche of British Petroleum by the UK government in October 1987. The price for the issue was set just before the stock market crash, and the underwriters (in particular the US underwriters, who were not able to sub-underwrite the majority of their allocation) were left with sizeable losses as the public refused to subscribe to the offer.

Third, since public offers aim to encourage the participation of retail investors, the marketing costs of such issues are often large. Many governments appear, however, to view such marketing as an investment in furthering a public policy goal of promoting wide share ownership.

As a result of these, and other, problems there has been a trend in recent years towards the use of multi-part offerings, with a public offer aimed at retail investors and a tender or book-building exercise aimed at larger investors. In such cases it has become normal for the public offer price to be set following the completion of the book-building or tender, which should allow for more accurate pricing. Typically, the public offer price would be set a little below the price established for institutional shareholders—to encourage wide share ownership—although other forms of incentives, such as bonus shares or reductions on bills, are frequently offered to retail investors.

Tenders Some privatizations (for example in France and some UK sales) have been conducted by means of a tender, which should, in principle, satisfy the revenue maximization objective. Pricing privatizations is no easy task, especially given the unique nature of many publicly held firms for whom there are few quoted private-sector firms that could be used as comparators to estimate their value. Tenders are a formal way of collecting the markets' collective estimate of the value of the assets, which should be superior to the estimate of any individual investment banker or public servant. However, it is notable that relatively few privatizations are in fact conducted by formal tenders, and, even where they are, the issues are sometimes still priced at a significant discount to the subsequent trading price.

An example of a procedure that was extremely efficient in maximizing revenue, and eliciting investors' valuations, was the tender component of the 1987 privatization of the British Airports Authority (BAA). In common with many recent UK privatizations, the IPO was split into separate parts: an offer for sale (for 75 per cent of the equity) aimed at individual shareholders, and a tender offer (for the remaining 25 per cent) aimed at institutional shareholders (although retail investors were not excluded). In the tender offer investors were invited to submit price/quantity bids. The interesting aspect of the tender was that those bids that were successful paid the price *bid*, rather than a common *strike price*. Essentially, the government was able to estimate the entire shape of the demand curve for the issue, and simply picked off the highest bids until all the shares on offer were allocated. In principle, this approach enables the vendor (in this case the government) to appropriate the entire 'consumers' surplus'. The result was that, while the fixed price offer was discounted by some 16 per cent, the average price paid under the tender offer was actually slightly higher than the trading price at the end of the first week.

While the BAA example is somewhat unusual in not setting a common strike price, the logic of trying to elicit information from market participants regarding their demand schedules before the issue price is set seems overwhelming. In practice, it is not necessary to sell the entire issue via a tender (which may be unattractive to relatively unsophisticated or uninformed investors); a partial tender, aimed at institutional investors, could be used to determine the issue price, with other techniques—such as offers for sale—used to sell the remainder. This approach was adopted by the Japanese government in the sale of Nippon Telegraph and Telecommunication (NTT), which involved an initial IPO by tender (restricted to institutions) for a relatively small proportion of the equity followed by subsequent secondary issues to which the public could subscribe. The later collapse of the NTT share price (and the large number of individual investors who incurred losses) should not detract from the attractiveness of such a procedure from the viewpoint of selling public assets at the correct price.

Book-building   A technique that has recently been introduced in a number of markets is book-building. As explained in Chapter 3, during a book-building exercise investors are invited to submit price/quantity bids for shares, with the co-ordinators of the book-building setting an indicative price range for the bids. Book-building is usually targeted at institutional investors. However, in many privatizations the co-ordinators also run a retail book to which individual investors can submit bids, although typically the minimum bid is significantly higher than that defined for the main public offer. There are clearly strong similarities between book-building and traditional tender offers— indeed, the book-building components of recent privatizations in Europe have often been referred to as 'international tender offers'— although the way in which the two techniques work differ in significant ways.

First, the type of bid that can typically be made in a book-building is very flexible. A bid could be for a fixed number of shares at a fixed price (as in a traditional tender), or the bid price could be expressed relative to a market index, or it could simply be for a fixed quantity of shares at whatever the eventual strike price is. Investors are also required to distinguish between firm bids and indicative bids. Having received all this information, the co-ordinators are then able to establish the likely shape of the entire demand curve and, it is argued, to price the issue accurately.

Second, the technique also allows considerable control over who is allocated shares. In the case of privatizations, governments will often give preferential treatment to investors who submit 'quality' bids. In practice, quality has a number of dimensions, including (i) bids that are firm rather than indicative; (ii) bids that are submitted early in the offer period (without such discrimination, investors would have an incentive to delay submitting their bids until the last minute to keep their options open, and hence little information would be forthcoming for the majority of the offer period); (iii) bids that are at a specific price (and so contribute to knowledge about the shape of the demand curve, unlike strike price bids); and (iv) bids that are from investors who are likely to be buyers in the after-market rather than sellers (in order to discriminate in favour of long-term investors rather than those hoping to stag the issue immediately, which might contribute to short-run price instability). The co-ordinators of the IPO are able to discriminate on this latter basis because banks (or other intermediaries) who participate in the IPO are required to disclose the identity of their clients.

Third, in practice a book-building exercise is often accompanied by a much more extensive marketing campaign than are traditional issues. This is, in part, because the returns from such efforts are potentially much greater. In a fixed price offering, once it is fully subscribed the only result of effective marketing is to contribute to over-subscription, which in the case of many privatizations has been extreme. However, in the case of book-building, where the price is not set until the last minute, successful marketing can result in a higher price being attained for the IPO, as increased demand will typically result in a higher price rather than greater rationing.

It is worth noting that the marketing mechanism, and the final allocations of shares, are often more informal in privatizations than is assumed in some of the theoretical models discussed in Chapter 3. (See, in particular, the discussion of the Benveniste–Spindt (1989) model.) In particular, the final share allocation is often determined by the government, not the co-ordinators. This implies that the latter cannot use the allocation mechanism to reward information production. In fact, the ubiquitous claw-back provisions—whereby institutional allocations are scaled down in the event of healthy retail demand—may be particularly problematic in this respect. If institutions truthfully reveal positive information about the privatization, this may encourage greater retail demand and hence, via the claw-back, smaller allocations for the institutions.

In the case of privatizations an important part of the marketing exercise is the provision of information to investors in foreign markets, to which flows of information through traditional channels may be relatively weak. Hence in the case of the privatization of Portugal Telecom in 1995, considerable interest developed during the latter stages of the book-building exercise from US investors who had become much more informed about the company, and about the Portuguese economy and stock market more generally, as a result of the efforts of the global co-ordinator Merrill Lynch and the syndicate of investment banks marketing the issue.

The marketing syndicate is often given strong incentives to market the issue effectively, although this may require careful structuring of commission arrangements. For example, in the USA it is commonplace for investors to book their sales through the global co-ordinator even if another member of the syndicate actually performed all the marketing to that particular investor. This is because there is often a belief that the chances of being allocated shares are higher if such a strategy is adopted. One way around this problem is to allow investors to designate to whom commission should be paid, which may or may not be the same syndicate member as receives the order. For example in the case of recent UK privatizations, 20 per cent of the commission has been designated as management commission payable to the syndicate to reflect fixed costs, while 80 per cent is related to business brought in. Investors designate which brokers should receive commission, and only successful allocations generate commission, so there is no advantage gained by bringing in lots of low-quality bids. The result has been strong incentives to perform the marketing, even if the sales are ultimately booked through the global co-ordinator. In the final stage of the British Telecommunications privatization in 1993, for example, S.G. Warburg—the global co-ordinator of the issue—generated 57 per cent of the allocations but received only 36 per cent of the selling commission.

Fourth, a key distinction between book-building and other forms of IPO is that underwriting commissions are avoided, as no fixed price is set until just before the shares are allocated. However, in place of underwriting commissions, there will be selling commissions to the syndicate to pay for the marketing of the issue. These can vary enormously according to the issue size. Jenkinson (1990) reports that the gross spread (reflecting the selling commissions) on private-sector IPOs in the USA ranged from nearly 10 per cent in the case of small issues to around 5 per cent on larger issues. However, privatizations are typically among the largest of IPOs, and so the associated commissions would be expected to be even lower. In the case of recent UK privatizations the selling commissions have been reduced to just 1 per cent, which compares favourably with those achieved elsewhere.

The main advantage of book-building, therefore, is that the issue is priced *after* a large quantity of information about demand for the shares has been gathered. In principle, this should allow the government to set the share price to approximately equate supply and demand. A subsidiary benefit is the control the process allows the government over the allocation of the available shares, with serious long-term investors being favoured over short-term speculative investors. Little of this information would be available in a traditional fixed-price offering.

However, despite the many positive aspects of book-building, in practice the results achieved are not always what one might expect from a technique that has a close similarity to a tender. Most noticeably, there are often very large discounts associated with book-building IPOs. One important reason for this is that the co-ordinators may set a price range that, in the event, turns out to be far too low. For example, in the flotation of the UK digital mobile phone operator Orange plc in 1996, the price range was set at 175p–205p. In the event there was considerable excess demand for the shares at the stated range—the issue was ten times subscribed—and the co-ordinators were left in the embarrassing position of setting the issue price at the top of the range and still seeing the trading price jump to 241p in initial trading.

Thus, while the book-building technique offers the *potential* for more accurate pricing, this will be contingent upon the correct price range being set in the first place. Of course, it would be possible to simply invite bids at any price, although in practice it may encourage greater participation in the offer to frame the question by indicating a range. The important lesson, however, is that one of the critical tasks of the global co-ordinators is accumulating enough information to set the price range appropriately, and to this extent the distinction between fixed price offers and book-building is rather less pronounced than it may first appear.

It could be argued, however, that the price range announced by the co-ordinators is only 'indicative' and that the final offer price could fall outside this range. This is certainly true, and in the USA issue prices above the upper bound are quite common in private-sector IPOs. However, practice in many other countries seems to be that prices below the lower bound are more common than prices above the upper bound. For example, in the case of the privatization of the Indonesian telecommunications company PT Telkom in November 1995, the indicative price range was set at US$19.50–US$24.50, with *eight* global co-ordinators charged with running the book. The government had initially planned to sell 70 million American depository shares (ADSs) in an international offer, but owing to weak demand scaled back the size of the issue to 30 million ADSs and cut the price to US$18. While many reasons were put forward for the lack of success of this book-building exercise, among the more convincing is the suggestion that having so many co-ordinators of an issue results in weakened incentives and poor leadership. As a result, the Indonesian government received a fraction of its desired revenue and lost some credibility in its on-going privatization programme.

A final point that should be noted regarding the book-building approach to IPOs is that, even after having gone through the extensive marketing and information gathering stages, governments frequently choose an issue price that generates considerable initial returns. Thus, the politics of privatization often conflicts with one of the main potential benefits of book-building, namely pricing IPOs more accurately.

7.2.2 Price stabilization

One of the interesting innovations that has recently been used in a number of privatizations in many countries is price stabilization. The form that this stabilization takes varies widely, ranging from intervention in the secondary market by the sponsor in the days or weeks immediately following the IPO to outright price guarantees by the government. In all cases, the main motivation is usually to attempt to reduce short-term share price volatility and in particular to reduce downside risk for investors. We consider in this section the various forms such stabilization can take.

Over-allotment options   The granting of a call option to the sponsor of an issue, whereby the sponsor is allowed to buy additional shares from the vendor (the government in the case of privatizations) at the issue price, is commonly known as an over-allotment option (or *Green Shoe*, after the US company that first granted such an option). Such options have been used extensively in the USA for many years, although only recently have they been utilized in Europe and elsewhere.

The purpose of the over-allotment option is as follows. If there is healthy demand for the shares at the time of the IPO, the sponsor can sell more shares than were allotted in the original offer, thus creating a short position. If prices in the after-market stay above the issue price, then no action is taken by the sponsor and the short position is covered by exercising the over-allotment option. Typically, the size of such options is 10–15 per cent of the issue size, although any sized option could be granted. However, the real purpose of the option is to reduce downward pressure on prices in the after-market. If the market price falls below the issue price, the sponsor will buy shares to partially, or fully, cover the short position. Since the sponsor purchases shares only at or below the offer price, covering the short position in this way is actually profitable. The ability of the sponsor to stabilize prices is limited by the size of the over-allotment option and the length of time over which the option is granted. A typical over-allotment may last for 30 days, although if the sponsor is confident that the share price will not fall the option may be exercised within this period.

Recent privatizations that have used over-allotment options include the second and third tranches of British Telecommunications (BT2 and BT3), and the second tranche of the UK electricity generators PowerGen and National Power (GenCo2). In the case of BT2 the over-allotment option was partially exercised, implying that some price stabilization occurred, whereas in the case of BT3 the option was exercised in full within the 30 day period covered by the option.

Probably the most interesting case is that of GenCo2. There was very strong demand for the issue, which was split between an offer for sale to the public and an international offer conducted by book-building, with the public offer being twice subscribed. The co-ordinators of the sale (Barclays de Zoete Wedd and Kleinwort Benson) took on a covered short position by selling 37 million additional shares in National Power and 24 million additional shares in PowerGen. Soon after the shares started trading, the UK electricity regulator, Professor Stephen Littlechild, announced that he was going to reopen a review of the prices that could be charged by electricity distribution companies. This announcement resulted in sharp falls in the shares of all companies in the electricity sector, even though the implications for the electricity generators were far from apparent. The GenCo shares rapidly fell to below their issue price, and the co-ordinators intervened in the market reducing excess supply and stabilizing the price. By the end of the 30-day option period, the co-ordinators were left with a short position totalling only 15.3 million shares, implying that they had repurchased 45.7 million shares in the market. In this case the volatility in the shares was genuinely short lived, as investors realized the limited impact the regulator's announcement would have on electricity generators, and the shares rapidly regained the initial losses and rose above the issue price.

One interesting aspect of this exercise is that it demonstrates how valuable the over-allotment option potentially is to the syndicate of investment banks selling the issue. Since they will buy back the shares in the market only if the price is below the issue price, in closing (partially or in full) their short position they make profits. These profits accrue to the syndicate itself, as the holder of the option, rather than to the government (or other vendors). Since such profits will be, in many cases, genuinely windfall, there is a strong case for writing contingencies into the underwriting contract to adjust the total remuneration of the syndicate in the event of profitable price stabilization. There are clearly many ways in which this could be done, ranging from an almost completely fixed price contract (where the total remuneration of the syndicate as a whole is fixed) to a system of claw-back of a proportion of any excess remuneration accruing from price stabilization. In the case of recent UK privatizations, the government has fixed a target income for the global co-ordinators and one-third of any excess income is clawed back. This preserves the incentives of the syndicate to intervene to stabilize the price. It could be argued, however, that, given the low cost of actually performing the price stabilization, the claw-back of this potential source of income for the syndicate should be much greater, or even complete. The provision of price support could be made part of the explicit contract, or implicitly agreed as in Germany. There seems little justification for the syndicate gaining once through additional selling commissions and then again through entirely risk-free repurchases at a lower price.

This episode illustrates some of the benefits to the vendor of over-allotment options, particularly in cases where there is short-run pressure on the share price. One obvious disadvantage is that granting such an option results in uncertainty as to the total revenue raised by the issue, as the initial owners will be left holding additional shares if the option is not exercised in full.

Price guarantees   Over-allotment options can certainly help in limiting short-run downward movements in share prices, and the provision of such (relatively limited) insurance should be valuable to risk averse investors. However, in some recent privatizations price stabilization has been extended to such lengths that some governments have actually started offering money-back guarantees within a given period. One recent example is Repsol, the Spanish oil group, which announced that, if its share price were to fall below the issue price in the year following the sale, it would compensate investors in cash for losses up to 10 per cent. Any fall in excess of 10 per cent would be borne by the investors.

While on first sight this approach seems a rather extreme form of insurance, from the perspective of the issuer it is similar to offering investors a one-for-ten bonus share issue, except that the bonus is not paid at all if the shares remain above the issue price, and will be paid only partially in the event of a fall of less than 10 per cent. Such bonus issues have been used extensively in privatizations in various countries, although in most cases the only contingency has been that the original investor has to retain ownership of the shares for some length of time, rather than being related to share price performance. The obvious advantage of the price guarantee variant of the scheme is that it will be a much cheaper way of providing insurance to risk averse retail investors than a simple bonus share scheme, as well as being more obviously risk-reducing to unsophisticated investors.

In the case of Repsol, a large tranche of shares were sold at a time (April 1995) when retail investors had suffered losses on the stock market both in general and in particular on previous privatization issues. For example, shares in Endesa, privatized less than a year previously, had fallen by around 20 per cent and shares in Argentaria, whose second—heavily oversubscribed—tranche had been issued just 16 months previously, had fallen by 35 per cent. The price guarantee certainly seemed to be effective, as the Repsol offer was heavily oversubscribed in both its domestic and international tranches. Most significant was the retail offer which was over twice subscribed.

The Spanish government seems to have used this issue to kick-start its remaining privatization programme by re-creating confidence—both among small shareholders and foreign investors—in the performance of privatization IPOs. Interestingly, the subsequent sale of part of the telecommunications group Telefonica by the Spanish government reverted to more traditional incentives—a discount to the institutional price for retail investors and a one-for-twenty bonus issue for those shareholders who retained their shares for one year.

Certainly the most astonishing example of a price guarantee is that apparently offered to the members of the employee stock ownership programme in the privatization of Deutsche Telekom planned for 1996. Not only will employees be protected from any decline in the share price, but their investments have also been leveraged (via the use of derivatives) to produce five times the gain in the share price during the six-year scheme. One rationale that has been suggested for this scheme is that it provides partial compensation to the employees of Deutsche Telekom, where around 40,000 jobs are expected to be lost in the first five years following privatization.

Hedging via the use of derivatives   The desire of governments to promote wide share ownership combined with the risk averse attitudes of many investors (especially following previous privatizations whose performance has been disappointing) has inevitably resulted in some intermediaries attempting to design schemes that hedge the downside risk. This is especially important in the case of employees of a privatizing company, as investing financial capital in addition to human capital in the same company can result in a very undiversified portfolio of assets. A downturn in the fortunes of the company could result in an increased chance of workers losing their jobs as well as a reduction in the value of their investments in the company. Since governments frequently seek to encourage employees to participate in a privatiz-ation, the attractions of offering a hedge—perhaps paid for in part by a less significant discount—can be considerable.

An example of the type of scheme that has been offered is that devised by Bankers Trust for the French government, which had been frustrated in its aim of encouraging more extensive employee partic-ipation in early privatizations. The scheme involved the government using part of the discount it would have offered to members of the em-ployee share ownership plan (ESOP) to buy a hedge against price falls, with the risk being taken on by Bankers Trust. The floor that was placed under the share price meant, in turn, that the shares could be used as collateral against a loan, which could be used to buy additional shares. For each share bought with their own money, investors could buy an additional nine with money borrowed from a bank, with Bankers Trust guaranteeing that the value of the shares would be sufficient to repay the loan. The cost to the members of the ESOP was that they received any share price appreciation on only six out of the ten shares, with the remainder going to Bankers Trust. However, the leveraged nature of the investment meant that potential returns were very high with no downside risk at all.

It should be clear that, although such schemes have initially been employed in privatization issues, the same techniques could potentially be used in a private-sector IPO, as in this case a financial intermediary is providing the price guarantee rather than the government. Although the idea of using derivatives to protect initial investors in an IPO is certainly relatively novel, such schemes may be a cheaper and more effective way of encouraging individual investors to participate in new issues, and it is possible that in the future initial underpricing may to some extent be replaced by such hedging, paid for in part by the company and in part by investors.

7.2.3 Part payment

A technique that has frequently been used in privatizations is that of selling shares on a partly paid basis. By allowing investors to pay only a proportion of the purchase price at the time of issue, the government essentially provides investors with free leverage to their holding. Put another way, the government provides investors with an interest-free loan for the period between the first instalment and the final instal-ment. Although the shares are traded on a partly paid basis, their volatility is far in excess of a fully paid equivalent, as is consistent with standard asset pricing models. For example, compare the behaviour of a fully paid share valued at 100p and a partly paid share in the same company with only half currently paid. Good results which increase the fully paid share price by 5 per cent to 105p will add the same absolute increase to the partly paid share price, which should rise from 50p to 55p, producing a 10 per cent return on the investment.

The advantage of employing such schemes from a government's perspective is that even relatively modest premia on privatization IPOs can become very impressive first day returns when the shares are issued on a partly paid basis. Part paid investors are also typically eligible to receive the full dividend, which can increase the yield on the partly paid shares dramatically. For investors wary of the stock market, governments often use such techniques to produce impressive initial returns, although more sophisticated investors should realize that they will subsequently have to pay the remaining instalments upon which there will be zero initial premium. None the less, the implicit interest-free loan is certainly an added inducement to invest, and the cost of providing such financing should essentially be viewed as additional implicit underpricing of the IPO.

However, there are possible disadvantages from using part payment schemes. Most significant is that it can encourage stagging, with investors able to reap impressive initial returns on the leveraged investment. Certainly, if the intention is to encourage retail investors to participate in the stock market in a long-term and responsible manner (rather than viewing new issues as a source of guaranteed profits), then part payment schemes appear much less appropriate than long-term incentive schemes. There are many variants of the latter, including bonus share schemes for retail investors who hold on to their initial holding for a set period of time, or discount schemes whereby investors receive discounts off their bills (often used in the case of utility privatizations). In some recent privatizations governments have adopted a belt-and-braces approach, offering both part payment and long-term incentives to retail investors. It remains to be seen if such schemes represent money well spent by government, which, as argued above, might be better advised to use such resources to encourage equity investment more generally, for example through the provision of tax exemptions on a certain amount of dividend income and capital gain accruing on equity investments.

Finally, it should be noted that in some recent privatizations governments have been prepared to price the subsequent instalments of the shares to reflect the benefits (in terms of leverage and yield) that investors receive from a part payment scheme. For example, in the sale of the second tranche of the UK electricity generators in 1995, the government issued the shares on a partly paid basis but set the subsequent instalments such that the fully paid price was around 6 per cent *above* the trading price of the existing fully paid equivalent shares. Individual investors were given a discount on the initial instalment in addition to bonus shares or additional discounts for those investors who had registered at 'Share Shops' by a particular date.

As the UK privatization programme has progressed, there has been an increasing use of incentives tied to establishing broker–investor relationships, which it is hoped will encourage investors to participate in equity investment more generally, rather than concentrating their attention on privatizations.

7.2.4 Staged sales

Given the problems that many governments have experienced in setting the correct price for privatizations, one obvious response is to conduct the sale in stages. A market price can be established on an initial tranche and subsequent tranches can be sold at more accurate prices later. Numerous governments have adopted the stage sale technique, although it is not always clear that revenue maximisation is the prime justification. We consider below some other objectives that might be achieved by the use of staged sales, but first draw attention to an important problem that can be encountered in using such a technique for privatizations.

Short sales When privatizations are conducted in stages, with the government attempting to encourage wide share ownership at each stage, a logical problem arises. Given that each tranche will be sold at a discount, with second and further tranches being sold at a discount to the market price, investors should sell their initial holding just before a further tranche is issued, as they can sell at the market price and then buy back at a discount to the market price. But this logic suggests that investors should, where possible, go further and short the issue (sell more shares than they own) and cover the short position by purchases in the next stage of the sale. There is evidence of this occurring in the USA (cf. Safieddine and Wilhelm 1996).

However, such behaviour by investors will tend to drive down the market price, which will reduce the revenue accruing to government from the sale of the remaining shares (which are offered at a discount to the market price). Indeed, this problem may be particularly acute during a book-building exercise, as it is in the interest of investors to drive the issue price down towards the bottom of the indicative range, only for the price to jump back up following the sale. There have been numerous examples of such problems in both private-sector secondary offerings and staged sale privatizations, including allegations of short-selling in the runup to the Eurotunnel and Wellcome secondary offerings in the UK.

There was also much concern at the time of the sale of the third tranche of British Telecommunications by the UK government in 1993, which illustrates graphically the potential problems posed by shorting. S.G. Warburg, the global co-ordinator of the book-building exercise, went to elaborate lengths to ensure that investors who shorted the shares before the offer were denied the opportunity to cover their positions by being allocated shares. Obviously, it is necessary either to have detailed information about share transactions around the time of the offering or to structure the rules regarding trading such that short sales are made less profitable. Both routes were attempted by the co-ordinators, which caused considerable friction with institutional investors. A report by the UK National Audit Office on the sale contains the remarkable fact that the Treasury asked financial regulators to give it information on the identity of those selling BT shares just before the issue, so that they could be denied allocations. However, lawyers advised that this would clearly be illegal and so other less direct methods were employed. The Stock Exchange undertook to monitor large transactions in BT shares just before the issue, and international investors were not told until the last minute how many shares they could buy (this being conditional upon domestic demand), thus making shorting more difficult. Warburg also asked the Stock Exchange to impose immediate cash settlement on BT shares in an attempt to reduce short sales, although the Stock Exchange decided against such a move.

In the event, the problems posed by short sales in this case seem not to have materialized, with the BT share price holding its value relative to the market between the date the sale was announced and the ultimate sale. However, governments considering staged sales should take such potential problems seriously. Various options, in addition to those employed above, exist to reduce such problems. For example, regulators could require the immediate publication of short sales in the period before a secondary sale, which would provide the co-ordinators with the required information to discriminate against those with short positions. Less extreme would be publication of the aggregate short position existing in the market as a whole, which could help the co-ordinators judge how much the current market price was being artificially depressed by such actions, and price the secondary offering accordingly. A final option might be to regulate short sales in some way, such as the US 'up-tick' rule, whereby short sales are allowed only when the last movement in the price was upwards. The problem, in any case, is likely to be less pronounced in markets where settlement occurs rapidly.

Wide share ownership   One important reason why governments are often attracted to staged sales is that wide share ownership can thereby be encouraged. Clearly, if individual investors are given significant incentives to apply for shares at each stage, this should increase their participation in the market. This will be particularly effective if the privatized company has performed strongly since privatization.

However, there is a more subtle reason for adopting staged sales if wide share ownership is a major policy goal. There is some evidence that the attrition rate of small shareholders is lower when the company is sold in stages. An interesting example is the case of British Telecommunications, which was sold in three stages in 1984, 1991, and 1993. After the IPO in 1984 the company had 2.1 million small shareholders, although this number fell to around 1 million within four years. The second stage of the privatization resulted in the number of small shareholders rising to 2.6 million, which fell to around 2.2 million before the sale of the final tranche. The 1993 offer increased the number of shareholders to 3.8 million, which by March 1994 had fallen to 2.7 million. Although these figures need to be interpreted with caution, as shareholder eligibility to incentives will have been an important determinant of the timing of sales, there is little doubt that by conducting the sale in stages the government has furthered the cause of wide share ownership. It may also be that the investors in the second and third stages of the sale will be longer term in nature, as staging profits are usually rather limited on secondary offerings.

Credibility   A final reason why staged sales may be employed for privatizations is to increase confidence in the minds of investors that the government will not change policy or intervene in ways that would harm the company and reduce shareholders returns. Although in principle privatization should mean the company being freed from government control, in practice many companies are still highly vulnerable to government policies. The most obvious example of such issues would be in the case of privatized utility industries, where governments typically establish regulatory agencies to control—at least—the natural monopoly activities of the privatized company. Although such regulators frequently have the appearance of being autonomous, governments are often able to influence decisions that directly impact on the profitability of the company in numerous ways. By retaining an equity stake in the company which will subsequently be sold, the government has a direct interest in maintaining the value of the company, at least for some time.

Although it is difficult to distinguish between credibility and commitment as the main reason for staged sales, it is remarkable how many privatizations have been conducted on this basis. For example, Chile set out a detailed schedule of when the various stages of its privatization plan would be executed for each company, which typically involved the sale of a minority stake followed by further sale(s) at regular intervals. Other countries prefer to sell a controlling stake at the IPO—to remove the worry that governments will still control the enterprise—followed by smaller staged sales.

7.3 Policy Conclusions

The previous two sections have discussed the main objectives of privatization, and the techniques that have been employed by many governments in achieving these various objectives. In this section we attempt to summarize how the various techniques and objectives relate to each other. We will illustrate the analysis using the example of the extensive UK privatization programme.

Table 7.2 shows, in broad terms, how the four main objectives of privatization are related to the various techniques available. Inevitably, the classification is subjective, and refers to broad experience across a number of countries rather than particular privatizations.

Table 7.2. Privatization objectives and techniques

Technique	Objective			
	Revenue maximization	Wide share ownership	Credibility	Control
Method of sale				
Public offers	✕	✓		✕
Tenders	✓	✕		?
Book-building	✓	✕		✓
Price stabilization				
Over-allotments	?			
Price guarantees	?	✓	✓	
Part payment	✕	?		
Staged sales	✓	✓	✓	?

7.3.1 Revenue maximization

In terms of the revenue maximisation objective, there is little doubt that methods involving a *tender* element (which includes book-building) have considerably more potential for reducing underpricing discounts and hence minimizing *ad hoc* transfers that can result from privatization programmes. Public offers, particularly when they are the sole method of sale, typically involve high discounts as risk averse governments, in possession of relatively little information regarding market demand, attempt to ensure that the shares go to a premium. However, it should be noted that large discounts are sometimes observed even when tenders or book-building are used. In part this may reflect the government's desire to promote wide share ownership, and could hence be viewed as voluntary. However, at times the initial indicative price range in a book-building exercise can be very wide of the mark, with actual demand being much greater than the co-ordinators anticipated. In this sense, book-building does not entirely remove the importance of establishing the correct price—in this case a price range—*a priori*.

Price stabilization techniques have ambiguous effects upon revenue maximization. The granting of over-allotment options introduces uncertainty into the final sum raised by the government. In the case of healthy demand the size of the issue can be increased, although it is not clear that this is necessarily in the government's interest, as presumably in this case the additional shares that they sell are likely to trade in the market at a premium to the offer price. To maximize revenue, the government should retain the shares and sell them later at the market price. In the case of price guarantees, these may be a relatively efficient way of encouraging wide share ownership, and can enable the government to reduce the discount on the IPO. They may also be a relatively cheaper way of providing longer-term incentives to hold the shares (relative to alternative schemes such as bonus shares) as they cost the government only in the event of share price falls.

Part payment is generally bad for revenue as the government essentially provides an interest-free loan over the instalment period. However, in some recent secondary offerings the UK government has actually been able to price partly paid shares at a premium over the fully paid price, which reduces the cost of providing such a facility, although it also raises the question as to why the government should provide loans for equity investment if they are undertaken on a commercial basis.

Staged sales are generally good for revenue in cases where the post-IPO share price performance is strong, as has often been the case. This is because subsequent tranches of the shares can be sold at higher market prices, and this seems a sensible approach for a government to take if there is a high degree of uncertainty regarding the fundamental value of the assets. Even in cases where the post-IPO performance is average, the discounts offered on secondary offerings are typically much smaller than those observed on privatization IPOs, which again should enhance revenue for the government.

7.3.2 Wide share ownership

The encouragement of wide share ownership will often result in a *public offer* being an important component of privatizations. Tenders and book-building are typically aimed at institutional investors, although it would be possible in countries with a developed system of retail brokers (such as the USA) for book-building to be compatible with the encouragement of small investors. *Price guarantees* are likely to be an effective way of encouraging retail investors, who are often both relatively risk averse and in possession of relatively undiversified portfolios. *Part payment* may encourage initial participation but, given that the opportunities for stagging profits are enhanced, may actually discourage the development of long-term shareholders. In contrast, *staged sales* may be a much more effective way of achieving wide share ownership, not only because the government has multiple bites at the same apple, but because there is some evidence that attrition rates for investors in secondary and further offerings are somewhat lower. Again, this is likely to be related to the lower discounts on offer, which discourage the stag and leave larger allocations available to investors with a longer time horizon.

7.3.3 Credibility

The credibility of a government's privatization programme is relatively difficult to establish and easy to lose. High IPO discounts on early privatizations are one of the most obvious (but relatively costly) means by which investors can be encouraged to participate in the programme of asset sales. However, credibility may also be enhanced by the use of *staged sales*, which result in the government retaining an equity interest in the company and hence reduce the incentives to *ex post* appropriation of shareholders' investment. *Price guarantees* may also help to establish, or re-establish, investor confidence, and can be seen as a risk-sharing contract between government and investor.

7.3.4 Control

The privatization process typically results in a change in the effective control of the company. The various methods of sale will have an important impact on how effective investor control is. *Public offers* will often result in a relatively diverse shareholder base which will tend to provide only weak control over management. *Tender offers* will generally be targeted at larger or institutional investors—who should provide more effective corporate control—although in most cases the government will actually have little information regarding the identity or intentions of the investors. In contrast, the *book-building* approach certainly provides the government with a much more detailed profile of the potential investors, and should enable discrimination towards investors with longer-term interests in the company and hence more commitment towards monitoring and controlling management.

Staged sales clearly provide the potential for government to retain a significant control over management (most obviously when the companies are still majority owned by the government). However, in practice many governments use such powers extremely sparingly, and some agree to a self-denying ordinance not to vote their shares. The relatively widespread use of special shares, which bestow control rights in certain circumstances, are likely to satisfy many governments' desires to retain a residual control over certain key industries but to withdraw from day-to-day management control.

To illustrate the problems of achieving these multiple, often conflicting, objectives in practice, it is interesting to take a closer look at the extensive privatization programme undertaken (and nearly completed) by the UK government. Table 7.3 details the method used in the IPO, the proportion sold at the IPO, the techniques used in secondary sales, whether an over-allotment option was granted, and whether the government retains a special share in the company.

As can be seen, many of the early privatizations in the UK adopted a very simple approach. Public offers, via offers for sale, were employed on all the main IPOs with the exception of two oil companies—Britoil and Enterprise Oil—which were sold by tender. Some of the initial returns recorded on these early offers for sale were spectacular. The British Telecom IPO, for example, was underpriced by some 33 per cent on a *fully paid basis*. Given that investors were also given the advantages of part payment, the short-term returns available to those staging the issue were as impressive as the revenue forgone by government.

It is interesting, however, that even quite early in the programme the government was experimenting with alternative methods of sale. The first attempt at tendering resulted in the Britoil issue being only 0.3 times subscribed, and the trading price for the shares falling to 20 per cent below the issue price. The tender of Enterprise Oil in 1984 was similar in that it was only 0.4 times subscribed, although the shares actually traded at a 2 per cent premium to the issue price by the end of the first week.

At the time of these early privatization tenders, it was quite common for private-sector companies to go public via a tender in the UK. However, virtually the last recorded tender in the UK was the sale of part of the British Airports Authority in 1987, which was discussed in some detail above. This was generally a highly successful attempt to maximize the proceeds, with healthy interest in the tender offer and an initial trading price exactly in line with the average price paid in the tender. It is unclear why this rather successful model was not adopted in the subsequent sales of British Steel, the 10 water companies, and the 12

Table 7.3. The UK privatization programme

Company	Date of IPO	Proceeds[a] (£m)	Technique	Proportion retained at IPO (%)	Staged sales 2nd tranche	3rd tranche	Special shares[d]
British Petroleum	11/79	284	OFS	51.0	9/81 T	10/87 OFS & T	
British Aerospace	2/81	43	OFS	48.4	5/85 OFS		Yes
Cable and Wireless	10/81	181	OFS	50.6	12/83 T	12/85 OFS	Yes
Amersham International	2/82	64	OFS	nil			
Britoil	10/82	334	T	49.0	8/95 OFS		
Assoc. British Ports	2/83	46	OFS	48.5	4/84 T		
Enterprise Oil	6/84	384	T	nil			
Jaguar[b]	7/84	297	OFS	nil			
British Telecom	11/84	3,685	OFS	49.8	12/91 OFS & BB; OAO	7/93 OFS & BB; OAO	Yes
British Gas	12/86	3,691	OFS	3.3	7/90 BD		Yes
British Airways	2/87	858	OFS	2.5			
Rolls Royce	5/87	1,032	OFS	0.4			Yes
British Airports Authority	7/87	1,223	OFS & T	4.4			Yes

British Steel	12/88	2,425	OFS	0.1		
10 Water Companies	12/89	3,395	OFS	1.6		
12 Regional Electricity Companies	12/90	3,395	OFS	1.5		
National Power	3/91	1,341	OFS & T^c	40.0	3/95 OFS & BB; OAO	Yes
PowerGen	3/91	822	OFS & T^c	40.0	3/95 OFS & BB; OAO	Yes
Scottish Hydro-Electric	6/91	920	OFS & T^c	3.5		Yes
Scottish Power	6/91	1,955	OFS & T^c	3.5		Yes
N. Ireland Electricity	6/93	684	OFS	3.3		Yes

Abbreviations: OFS: offer for sale at a fixed price; T: tender; BB: book-building; BD: bought deal; OAO: over-allotment option granted.

[a] The proceeds figures include the value of the sale of ordinary shares at the IPO but do not include the value of any debt or preference shares created in the company that are repayable to the government, or the proceeds from the second and third tranches of staged sales.

[b] In the case of Jaguar, the proceeds of the sale were retained by its parent company (British Leyland).

[c] In these cases the tenders were 'back-end' tenders.

[d] Only special shares that are still in place are noted here. Some special shares were created that expired at certain dates (such as the water companies and the regional electricity companies); others (such as in the case of Jaguar) were redeemed at the time of a takeover.

Source: HM Treasury (1995)

regional electricity companies. While the former was priced relatively accurately, the latter two issues were significantly underpriced, with end of first week share price rises of 22 and 21 per cent respectively, again on a fully paid basis. The loss of potential revenue in these two cases was made worse by the fact that not only were the sales not staged, but the longer-term performance of the companies has been exceptionally strong. In cases where information regarding the true value of the company is sparse, there are very strong arguments in favour of staged sales.

A major criticism we would make of the UK privatization programme is that the relative neglect of the benefits of staged sales was a costly mistake, and one that was repeated in the 1996 sale of Railtrack, the UK rail network operator. Political considerations may well have dominated economic argument in this respect, with the government keen to sell its entire stake in order that any future government of a different complexion would find it more difficult to reverse the privatization or seize effective control by re-establishing majority control.

Around 1991 the UK government started to use book-building techniques, which it has employed in the secondary offerings of BT, PowerGen, and National Power. It has also used book-building for the Railtrack offering. The approach has been to segment the offer into a public offer, an international tender offer (conducted by book-building), and, in more recent offers, a retail tender aimed at relatively sophisticated individual investors who want to increase their allocation over and above what they might receive through the public offer. The public offer price has been set at a fixed discount to the price established through the book-building exercise. This approach seems much more sensible than the offer for sale route, where the government, in its desire to encourage wide share ownership, discounted the shares to both individuals and institutions alike.

Special shares have been widely employed in UK privatizations, as can be seen in the final column of Table 7.3. This shows the special shares that are currently in existence; in fact, a number of the other companies—such as the water companies and regional electricity companies—also had special shares in place that have since expired. In practice, the UK government has on a number of occasions waived its control rights, and allowed several mergers and acquisitions to occur. It did, however, use its veto in 1996 to block the attempt by a US electricity utility to take over National Power, the largest UK generating company.

Price stabilization has taken place only in a few recent sales, and has taken the form of the granting of over-allotment options. The benefits to the government, or investors, of the existence of these options seem rather marginal, although it could be argued that they contribute to price stability in the initial trading period. What is clear is that the remuneration contract of the co-ordinators who are granted these options should be carefully written, as potentially such options are highly profitable. However, claw-back by the government of any profits resulting from price stabilization (carried out in the security of a covered short position) may be politically sensitive, as the government would essentially be profiting directly from the losses incurred by the initial investors.

Price guarantees, which are being used quite widely in other European countries, have not been used in the UK, where bonus share allocations and other incentives—such as reduced bills—have been the main form of long-term incentive. However, as argued above, there are good arguments for partial price guarantees which may be a more effective and cheaper way of encouraging wide share ownership.

In conclusion, this chapter has discussed the various objectives of privatization programmes and the techniques available to government. Many of the issues are similar to those facing a private-sector company conducting an IPO, although there are significant differences, not least the fact that governments have many companies to sell and so return to the market on numerous occasions. What is clear is that the simple public offer of shares is becoming much less common, with more sophisticated methods such as book-building tending to play a more prominent role. There is also likely to be a more extensive use of derivatives to provide hedging or price guarantees to investors, with a proportion of the cost of such support being borne by the government. In general, we have tended to stress the relative importance of revenue raising, and suggested that wide share ownership as a public policy objective is poorly defined and may be more appropriately achieved through means other than a privatization programme.

8

CONCLUSIONS AND FUTURE DEVELOPMENTS

....

Whenever economists find an empirical anomaly, a sizeable theoretical literature usually develops. In the case of initial public offerings, there are not one but two anomalies: initial underpricing and long-run underperformance. It is not surprising, therefore, that the resultant theoretical and empirical literature is so extensive. However, at present, the bulk of the theoretical explanations have been associated with underpricing. In part this is simply because underpricing is such a long established international stylized fact; papers on long-run under-performance only (re)appeared in journals around 1991.[1] However, it is also true that the empirical support for long-run underperformance is not nearly as clear cut. We suspect that as research proliferates in this area additional doubts may well emerge as to the validity of the claim that IPOs underperform the relevant benchmark in the long run.

One of the principal aims of this book has been to provide a critical assessment of the plausibility of the alternative theories that attempt to explain these phenomena, drawing in particular upon international evidence. The international perspective is especially valuable in that it allows explanations based upon particular institutional, legal, or regu-latory arrangements to be tested. Initial underpricing is truly an inter-national stylized fact, but the financial systems in which it is observed differ greatly. While in many papers evidence has been presented for particular countries (especially the USA) that is claimed to be 'con-sistent' with particular theories, it is clear from Part II of this book that

---

[1] As in many other areas of economics, an earlier literature existed on long-run under-performance; see for example Stoll and Curley (1970). However, the recent resurgence in research activity in this area really dates from the 1990s.

few theories could claim to provide a convincing international explanation of underpricing. As a result, any theory whose conclusions are dependent on a restrictive set of assumptions about financial institutions or company law is likely to lack general validity or plausibility.

In this final chapter we first review the state of the theoretical debate in this spirit, suggesting which classes of theory provide the most insights. We finish by speculating on possible future developments in the way firms go public.

8.1 An Assessment of the Theoretical Literature

Of the theoretical explanations of underpricing, we find those based upon the assumption of information asymmetries most convincing. However, this is not to say that all of the theories in this relatively large class are equally compelling. In particular, while we believe that principal–agent and marketing explanations have quite general plausibility, we are much less convinced of the relevance of winner's curse explanations except in cases where the owners of the company have strong desires to encourage small investors to participate in the flotation. Clearly, the most obvious such cases have been privatization IPOs in many countries. We are less convinced still of signalling explanations. We briefly discuss below the reasons for these views.

Companies go public once only, and so for this reason there is obviously a role for intermediaries who repeatedly sponsor new companies, who have reputations to preserve, and who have established clienteles for the shares of new companies. The typical issuing company is likely to be better informed about its own business and prospects, but in other respects is likely to be at an informational disadvantage relative to the investment bank, particularly regarding likely investor demand. There are, as a result, numerous ways in which the interests of intermediaries and companies may not always be perfectly aligned, resulting in potential principal–agent problems.

Most obviously, in cases where the issue is underwritten by an investment bank, the latter will have an incentive to reduce its underwriting risk by increasing the extent of (expected) underpricing. Similarly, it becomes easier to sell future issues to repeat investors if previous issues have been underpriced. While such explanations lack the complexity of other principal–agent models, we believe they should not be discarded lightly. However, there are other more sophisticated principal–agent explanations, for example where underpricing emerges as a second-best incentive-compatible contract between the issuer and bank.

In the case of IPOs conducted by book-building—a long established method in the USA that is becoming increasingly common in Europe and elsewhere—there may be additional informational problems. Book-building involves two stages: the information gathering stage, followed by the pricing and selling stage. If some investors are more informed than others about the prospects for the company going public, why should they reveal this information to the bank running the book? After all, if they have positive information about the company, they will tend to bid up the price against themselves. Theories that explain how underpricing and rationing can be used to devise a mechanism that ensures truthful revelation of information during the marketing stage seem particularly pertinent. It should be noted, however, that book-building techniques are not used, or have only just been introduced, in many countries, so these marketing theories are not relevant for a sizeable proportion of IPOs.

Probably the most widely cited theory of IPO underpricing is that of the winner's curse. This is also an asymmetric information theory, although the nature of the information asymmetry is of a very different nature. Some investors are assumed to be relatively more informed than others, but both the issuing firm and its investment bank are assumed to be equally uninformed. There are, as a result, no principal–agent problems in the winner's curse theory, and, indeed, the investment bank plays no particular role.

We do not find these assumptions regarding the nature of the asymmetric information problem very convincing, but even if they are accepted, a major problem with winner's curse explanations is that it is unclear why companies need to attract these persistently 'uninformed' investors. In some countries small shareholders (who are likely to be relatively uninformed on average) have never participated to any great extent in IPOs, and even in countries with active retail sectors many companies completely ignore them (for example, through private placements). We still observe underpricing in these situations. The winner's curse model relies upon an assumption that without the uninformed investors' participation there would be insufficient demand for the shares; in an increasingly global capital market, we find this hard to believe.

Winner's curse theories seem most relevant in those cases where the original owners want to encourage wide share ownership. The most obvious cases where this may apply are privatizations, although we suggested in the previous chapter that promoting wide share ownership through underpriced privatizations may be both ineffective and costly. However, theories based upon the importance of corporate control—which we discussed in Chapter 5—also suggest that the original owner/managers may value a wide initial shareholder base. While we believe these latter, relatively recent, theories are at best of only limited relevance, if, for whatever reason, wide share ownership is an objective of the initial owners, then the winner's curse is likely to be relevant in such cases.

Among the explanations that are not based upon asymmetric information, we find those associated with price support most convincing. The quite widespread use of various techniques to limit price falls in the after-market, at least for a short period of time, may well help to explain the observed extent of underpricing. Since initial underpricing is typically measured over a short period—such as the first trading week—during which intermediaries may be intervening in the market to bolster demand, there may be a sense in which such initial trading prices do not accurately reflect underlying market prices. This is likely to be most important for those issues whose initial trading prices are close to, or below, the issue price, since intervention will be heaviest in these cases.

The effect of such price support may be to result in a distribution of initial discounts that is artificially truncated on one side—with fewer overpriced issues than would be observed in the absence of such intervention. As a result, estimates of average initial underpricing may be somewhat misleading. It is also clear that such explanations may go some way to explaining the apparent long-run underperformance of IPOs, although how significant such effects are remains to be tested.

We turn now to the theories that we view as less convincing. Despite the proliferation of models suggesting a signalling explanation for IPO underpricing, we find these an implausible set of theories. There is clearly something in the argument that companies do not want to overprice their IPOs as investors may remember and subsequently not subscribe to secondary equity offerings. Indeed, more generally, companies may want to avoid the 'bad publicity' of an overpriced issue, although to a great extent the blame ought to attach to the investment bank conducting the sale. However, this does not imply that initial underpricing is the most likely way for companies to signal their quality. Indeed, even the previous argument is questionable—since bygones should be bygones for investors, it is not clear why it is rational to boycott a secondary offering if the primary offering was overpriced.

While there is some evidence from the USA that is 'consistent' with the models, in many other countries the institutional arrangements are such as to make the models completely irrelevant—notably those countries where investors enjoy pre-emption rights. In any case, the models are often based upon very questionable assumptions—for example, that companies require equity, rather than other forms of finance, to get going in the first place.

Similarly, we find little general relevance in the theories that stress the role of underpricing in reducing the threat of legal action. While such theories may have some relevance to the USA we have argued that the far greater protection afforded to intermediaries and issuing companies in most other countries renders such explanations of very limited relevance.

Finally, a relatively new set of explanations points to the possible links between initial underpricing and ownership and control. The models that have been proposed suggest that the principal–agent problem is between managers and shareholders. However, the relationship between underpricing and such agency costs is currently the subject of much unresolved debate. One theory suggests that underpricing, via the attendant over-subscription and the power to ration bids, results in dispersed shareholdings and the entrenchment of management control. An alternative theory suggests quite the opposite: that underpricing may be used to minimize agency costs by encouraging monitoring. At present this literature is relatively speculative and in need of more powerful empirical tests of its validity.

8.2 Possible Future Developments

The previous brief summary of the theoretical literature showed that, to some extent, underpricing may result from incomplete contracts between the various parties to the transaction. The company going public may typically want to be sold at a modest discount to the resulting trading price in order to avoid both the bad publicity and the initial disgruntled set of shareholders that might result from an overpriced issue. At the same time, the company may want to give strong incentives to its investment bank to market the issue vigorously, achieve a high sale price, and avoid excessive underpricing. Investors, who may be the least informed party to the transaction, may value some implicit or explicit insurance against possible price falls.

Existing examples of some implicit guarantees on price include the growing use of price support often covered by the granting of over-allotment options. This provides a good illustration of how important it is to write an appropriate contract. Granting an over-allotment option has a complex effect upon incentives. On the one hand, doing so may be rational for the issuing company as it should reduce the incentive for the investment bank to underprice. This is because the syndicate banks profit if the trading price falls below the issue price and they are able to cover their short position by purchases in the market at below the price they received for the shares. On the other hand, if the syndicate does sell additional shares, selling commissions will increase. Since many of the costs of marketing are to a great extent fixed, the profitability of additional marginal sales will usually be high for the syndicate.

We remain to be convinced of the attractions of over-allotment options for companies going public. However, since these are potentially valuable options that are granted to the selling syndicate, companies should certainly define the terms of the contract carefully. For example, in the event that the trading price does fall below the issue price, the issuing firm should, surely, have a provision in its contract whereby it claws back a large proportion of the profits that would otherwise accrue to the syndicate. Another clause that might be considered is to reduce the marginal selling commission on over-allotted shares, so that the underpricing incentives for the syndicate are reduced.

There are also various ways to align the incentives of the issuing company and the investment bank. For example, a relatively simple innovation (that we have never heard of in practice) would be to make the investment banks' fees contingent on underpricing not being 'excessive'. Investors require encouragement to participate in the IPO rather than invest in the after-market, and so a company might have a target level of underpricing of, say, 0%–5%. Underpricing in excess of this could result in a reduction in the fees paid to the investment bank on a sliding scale basis. In principle, a highly underpriced issue could result in the investment bank actually paying money to the company, rather than *vice versa*. In this way, the investment bank would share in the 'success' of the issue, where success is as defined by the *company*, rather than by the intermediaries—who traditionally herald a hugely over-subscribed and underpriced issue as a success.

Of course, as investment banks are the repeat players, one might expect that—in a competitive market—previous history on under-pricing would be taken into account when deciding which under-writer/manager to choose. Intermediaries that had been associated historically with highly underpriced issues would be avoided by companies; those that had overpriced previous issues would be avoided by investors. Consequently, a rational strategy for an investment bank might be to aim to be *average*—at least in terms of underpricing—and various investment banks have actually suggested to us that this is indeed their aim.

However, while reputations based upon past performance are clearly important, they are not the same as proper financial instruments. We believe that in the future there will be significant innovations in the way IPOs are sold, making much more extensive use of derivatives contracts. We have already started seeing such innovations in the case of privatizations, with options being used to provide downside in-surance and/or leverage potential gains. There is no reason why such contracts might not be written for private-sector IPOs. For example, an intermediary might guarantee that the share price would not fall below a specified level over a particular period. As we have seen in the case of some French privatizations, such a guarantee would enable investors to leverage up their positions with the cost of the hedge being paid for—in part or in full—by forgoing upside returns.

Such a scheme would be a familiar 'cap and collar' arrangement which would truncate the possible returns at both ends of the distri-bution. Risk averse, and possibly informationally disadvantaged, in-vestors might be especially attracted to such schemes, and companies might find them a cheaper and more effective way of attracting investors, thus lowering the cost of equity capital.

Indeed, the use of such instruments may provide a quick way for new entry to occur by intermediaries who lack established reputations for sponsoring IPOs, as investors care less about reputations when they are offered explicit financial deals (as witnessed by the growth of various forms of guaranteed income bonds with upside potential engineered using derivatives). What would still matter, of course, was that the financial instruments backing up the package were adequately secured, although in practice positions would probably be substan-tially hedged.

In principle, it is even possible for the company itself, or more accurately the initial owners of the company, to offer price guarantees. There have been examples in the USA of the use of 'puttable stock' whereby investors are sold a unit comprising a share of common stock and an option provided by the issuing company (see the examples cited in Chen and Kensinger 1988). The option gives the unit-holder the right at a predetermined time to claim more stock (or, possibly, cash or other securities) if the market price has fallen below a specified level. If the market value of the shares rises above this level, the option becomes worthless and is not exercised. If the share price has fallen below the guaranteed level at the relevant date, the original investors (whose shares were not sold in the IPO) will see the value of their shares fall, as the IPO shareholders are compensated. Clearly, if the company experienced really hard times, complete dilution of the original investors' stakes might be insufficient to cover the cost of the guarantee, which necessitates a supplementary mechanism for entering bankruptcy.

There are close analogies between puttable stock and convertible bonds, as both types of security allow investors to share in the upside gains while downside risk is limited. This is an example of *disintermediation*. (Although, clearly, intermediaries may be involved in the initial design of such schemes, they do not bear the risk or necessarily put their reputation on the line.)

Another interesting example of disintermediation can be seen when companies choose to separate the establishment of a stock market quotation from the raising of equity finance. All stock exchanges have requirements that the shares of companies should be reasonably widely held before they are quoted on the exchange (in order to ensure after-market liquidity). In many cases a company will achieve such dispersed ownership via an initial public offering. However, many companies that go public actually satisfy such dispersed ownership criteria before the IPO. One option that is available to such companies is to obtain a stock exchange listing *before* raising additional equity finance or the original owners sell some of their stakes. In this way the underpricing cost of conducting an IPO would be avoided. Of course, one disadvantage of such an approach is that the proceeds to original shareholders who want to reduce their stakes would not be known for certain, as they would depend upon the trading price established in the after-market. However, although an underwritten IPO will guarantee a particular price, history shows that the cost of such insurance is high, consisting of both the underwriting commissions and the underpricing.

Examples of such two-stage strategies can be found in the UK, where the act of obtaining a stock market quotation without raising money is known as an *introduction*. While introductions have been quite widely used in recent years, they have not yet been the subject of academic attention. It would be interesting to observe whether separating capital-raising from the establishment of a share price is an effective way of overcoming the initial underpricing problem. It would also be interesting to observe whether such companies were also the subject of long-run underperformance.

In conclusion, we envisage important developments in the way companies raise initial equity finance in future years. In many countries the established system of going public is very far from best practice. One reason for this is that the market for intermediaries—who put their reputation (and, in some cases, selling power) behind IPOs—is often highly uncompetitive. Capital markets are rapidly becoming more integrated. For example, stock exchanges now compete vigorously with each other for new companies; national prejudices are disappearing fast. We expect, therefore, to see both an increase in competition between intermediaries and a convergence towards those techniques that most effectively overcome the information problems inherent in most IPOs. We also expect to see the development of contracts that more accurately align the interests of the various parties to the transaction. We have speculated that a greater role may be played by derivative securities in packaging IPOs in the future and that such developments could fundamentally alter the role of intermediaries. In certain circumstances, we can even envisage a trend towards disintermediation. However, our firmest prediction is that initial public offerings will continue to be the subject of intense academic debate. Whether this research activity produces more convincing—and internationally relevant—explanations for the two apparent anomalies of initial underpricing and long-run underperformance remains to be seen.

REFERENCES

Affleck-Graves, J. and M. J. Page, 1995, 'The Timing and Subsequent Performance of Seasoned Offerings: The Case of Rights Issues', mimeo, University of Notre Dame, IN.
—— and D. K. Spiess, 1995, 'Underperformance in Long-Run Stock Returns Following Seasoned Equity Offerings', *Journal of Financial Economics* 38, 243–267.
Aggarwal, R. and P. Rivoli, 1990, 'Fads in the Initial Public Offering Market?' *Financial Management* 19, 45–57.
—— R. Leal, and L. Hernandez, 1993, 'The After-Market Performance of Initial Public Offerings in Latin America', *Financial Management* 22, 42–53.
Akerlof, G., 1970, 'The Market for "Lemons": Quality Uncertainty and the Market Mechanism', *Quarterly Journal of Economics* 84, 488–500.
Alexander, J. C., 1993, 'The Lawsuit Avoidance Theory of Why Initial Public Offerings Are Underpriced', *UCLA Law Review* 17, 17–73.
Ali, A., 1995, 'Bias in Analysts' Earnings Forecasts as an Explanation for the Long-Run Underperformance of Stocks Following Equity Offerings', mimeo, University of Arizona, Tucson.
Allen, F. and G. R. Faulhaber, 1989, 'Signaling by Underpricing in the IPO Market', *Journal of Financial Economics* 23, 303–323.
Alphao, R. M., 1989, 'Initial Public Offerings on the Lisbon Stock Exchange', mimeo, Faculdade de Economia, Universidade Nova de Lisboa.
Asquith, D., J. D. Jones, and R. Kieschnick, 1995, 'Price Stabilisation and Underpricing of IPOs: A Mixture of Distributions Perspective', mimeo, Federal Communications Commission, Washington, DC.
Balvers, R. J., B. McDonald, and R. E. Miller, 1988, 'Underpricing of New Issues and the Choice of Auditor as a Signal of Investment Banker Reputation', *Accounting Review* 63, 605–622.
Barber, B. M. and J. D. Lyon, 1995, 'Detecting Long-Run Abnormal Stock Returns: The Empirical Power and Specification of Test Statistics', mimeo, University of California, Davis.
Baron, D. P., 1982, 'A Model of the Demand for Investment Banking Advising and Distribution Services for New Issues', *Journal of Finance* 37, 955–976.
—— and B. Holmström, 1980, 'The Investment Banking Contract for New Issues under Asymmetric Information: Delegation and the Incentive Problem', *Journal of Finance* 35, 1115–1138.

Barry, C. B., C. J. Muscarella , J. W. Peavy, and M. R. Vetsuypens, 1990, 'The Role of Venture Capital in the Creation of Public Companies: Evidence from the Going-Public Process', *Journal of Financial Economics* 27, 447–471.

Beatty, R. P., 1989, 'Auditor Reputation and the Pricing of Initial Public Offerings', *Accounting Review* 64, 693–709.

—— and J. R. Ritter, 1986, 'Investment Banking, Reputation, and the Underpricing of Initial Public Offerings', *Journal of Financial Economics* 15, 213–232.

—— E. J. Zajac, 1995, 'Managerial Incentives, Monitoring and Risk Bearing in Initial Public Offering Firms', *Journal of Applied Corporate Finance* 8, 87–96.

Beller, A. L., T. Terai, and R. M. Levine, 1992, 'Looks Can Be Deceiving: A Comparison of Initial Public Offering Procedures under Japanese and US Securities Laws', *Law and Contemporary Problems* 55, 77–118.

Benveniste, L. M. and P. A. Spindt, 1989, 'How Investment Bankers Determine the Offer Price and Allocation of New Issues', *Journal of Financial Economics* 24, 343–361.

—— and W. J. Wilhelm, 1990, 'A Comparative Analysis of IPO Proceeds under Alternative Regulatory Environments', *Journal of Financial Economics* 28, 173–207.

—— W. Busaba, and W. J. Wilhelm, 1995, 'Price Stabilisation as a Bonding Mechanism in new Equity Issues', mimeo, Boston College, MA.

Booth, J. R. and L. Chua, 1996, 'Ownership Dispersion, Costly Information and IPO Underpricing', *Journal of Financial Economics* 41, 291–310.

—— and R. Smith, 1986, 'Capital Raising, Underwriting and the Certification Hypothesis', *Journal of Financial Economics* 15, 261–281.

Brealey, R. A. and S. C. Myers, 1991, *Principles of Corporate Finance*, 4th edn. New York: McGraw-Hill.

Brennan, M. J. and J. Franks, 1995, 'Underpricing, Ownership and Control in Initial Public Offerings of Equity Securities in the UK', CEPR Discussion Paper No. 1211, London.

Buijs, A. and H. G. Eijgenhuijsen, 1993, 'Initial Public Offerings in the Netherlands 1982–1991: An Analysis of Initial Returns and Long-Run Performance', mimeo, Free University of Amsterdam.

Burkart, M., D. Gromb, and F. Panunzi, 1995, 'Large Shareholders, Monitoring and the Value of the Firm', Discussion Paper No. 220, London School of Economics.

Cai, J. and K. C. J. Wei, 1996, 'The Investment and Operating Performance of Japanese IPO Firms', mimeo, Hong Kong University of Science and Technology.

Carter, R. B. and S. Manaster, 1990, 'Initial Public Offerings and Underwriter Reputation', *Journal of Finance* 45, 1045–1067.

Chemmanur, T. J., 1993, 'The Pricing of Initial Public Offerings: A Dynamic Model with Information Production', *Journal of Finance* 48, 285–304.

Chen, A. H. and J. W. Kensinger, 1988, 'Puttable Stock: A New Innovation in Equity Financing', *Financial Management* 17, 27–37.

Chen, H. L., 1992, 'The Price Behaviour of IPOs in Taiwan', mimeo, University of Illinois.

Cheng, L.-L., 1996, 'Equity Issue Under-Performance and the Timing of Security Issues', mimeo, National Economic Research Associates, White Plains, NY.

Cherubini, U. and M. Ratti, 1992, 'Underpricing of Initial Public Offerings in the Milan Stock Exchange, 1985–91', mimeo, Banca Commerciale Italiana.

Cheung, Y.-L., S. L. Cheung, and R. Y.-K. Ho, 1993, 'Listing Requirements, Uncertainty, and Underpricing of IPOs', mimeo, City Polytechnic of Hong Kong.

Chowdhry, B. and V. Nanda, forthcoming, 'Stabilisation, Syndication, and Pricing of IPOs', Journal of Financial and Quantitative Analysis.

Clarkson, P. M. and J. Merkley, 1994, 'Ex Ante Uncertainty and the Underpricing of Initial Public Offerings: Further Canadian Evidence', Canadian Journal of Administrative Sciences 11, 54–67.

—— and R. Thompson, 1990, 'Empirical Estimates of Beta When Investors Face Estimation Risk', Journal of Finance 45, 431–453.

Cusatis, P. J., J. A. Miles, and J. R. Woolridge, 1993, 'Restructuring through Spinoffs: The Stock Market Evidence', Journal of Financial Economics 33, 293–311.

Davis, E. W. and K. A. Yeomans, 1976, 'Market Discount on New Issues of Equity: The Influence of Firm Size, Method of Issue and Market Volatility', Journal of Business Finance and Accounting 3, 27–42.

Dawson, S. M., 1987, 'Secondary Stock Market Performance of Initial Public Offers, Hong Kong, Singapore and Malaysia: 1978–84', Journal of Business Finance and Accounting 14, 65–76.

DeAngelo, H. and E. Rice, 1983, 'Anti-Takeover Charter Amendments and Stockholder Wealth', Journal of Financial Economics 11, 329–360.

DeGeorge, F. and R. Zeckhauser, 1993, 'The Reverse LBO Decision and Firm Performance: Theory and Evidence', Journal of Finance 48, 1323–1348.

Dhatt, M. S., Y. H. Kim, and U. Lim, 1993, 'The Short-Run and Long-Run Performance of Korean IPOs: 1980–90', mimeo, University of Cincinnati.

Drake, P. D. and M. R. Vetsuypens, 1993, 'IPO Underpricing and Insurance against Legal Liability', Financial Management 22, 64–73.

Dunbar, C. G., 1995, 'The Use of Warrants as Underwriter Compensation in Initial Public Offerings', Journal of Financial Economics 38, 59–78.

Fama, E. F. and K. R. French, 1992, 'The Cross-Section of Expected Stock Returns', Journal of Finance 47, 427–465.

Fernandez, P., E. Martinez-Abascal, and A. Rahnema, 1992, 'Initial Public Offerings: The Spanish Experience', mimeo, IESE.

Field, L. C., 1995, 'Is Institutional Investment in Initial Public Offerings Related to Long-Run Performance of These Firms?', mimeo, University of California, Los Angeles.

Finn, F. J. and R. Higham, 1988, 'The Performance of Unseasoned New Equity Issues-cum-Stock Exchange Listings in Australia', Journal of Banking and Finance 12, 333–351.

Garfinkel, J. A., 1993, 'IPO Underpricing, Insider Selling and Subsequent Equity

Offerings: Is Underpricing a Signal of Quality?' *Financial Management* 22, 74–83.

Göppl, H. and A. Sauer, 1990, 'Die Bewertung von Börsenneulingen am deutschen Aktienmarkt: Eine empirische Notiz', in W. R. Heilmann *et al.* (eds.), *Geld, Banken und Versicherungen*, vol. 1. Karlsruhe: VVW.

Goergen, M. G. J., 1995, 'The Evolution of Ownership and Control in German Corporations: A Dynamic Analysis', mimeo, Keble College Oxford.

Grinblatt, M. and C. Y. Hwang, 1989, 'Signalling and the Pricing of New Issues', *Journal of Finance* 44, 393–420.

Grossman, S. and O. Hart, 1980, 'Takeover Bids, the Free-Rider Problem and the Theory of the Corporation', *Bell Journal of Economics* 11, 42–64.

Guney, S. E. and E. C. Perotti, 1993, 'The Structure of Privatisation Plans', *Financial Management* 22, 84–98.

Hanley, K. W. and J. R. Ritter, 1992, 'Going Public', in J. Eatwell, M. Milgate and P. Newman (eds.), *The New Palgrave Dictionary of Money and Finance*. London: Macmillan.

Helwege, J. and N. Liang, 1996, 'Is There a Pecking Order? Evidence from a Panel of IPO Firms', *Journal of Financial Economics* 40, 429–458.

Hin, T. C. and H. Mahmood, 1993, 'The Long-Run Performance of Initial Public Offerings in Singapore', *Securities Industry Review* 19, 47–58.

H.M. Treasury, 1995, *Her Majesty's Treasury Guide to the UK Privatisation Programme*. London: HMSO.

Högholm, K. and K. Rydqvist, forthcoming, 'Going Public in the 1980s: Evidence from Sweden', *European Financial Management*.

Hughes, P. J. and A. V. Thakor, 1992, 'Litigation Risk, Intermediation, and the Underpricing of Initial Public Offerings', *Review of Financial Studies* 5, 709–742.

Husson, B. and B. Jacquillat, 1989, 'French New Issues, Underpricing and Alternative Methods of Distribution', in R. M. C. Guimaraes, B. G. Kingsman, and S. J. Taylor (eds.), *A Reappraisal of the Efficiency of Financial Markets*. Berlin, Heidelberg: Springer-Verlag.

Ibbotson, R. G., 1975, 'Price Performance of Common Stock New Issues', *Journal of Financial Economics* 2, 235–272.

—— and J. F. Jaffe, 1975, ' "Hot Issue" Markets', *Journal of Finance* 30, 1027–1042.

—— J. R. Ritter, and J. L. Sindelar, 1994, 'The Market's Problems with the Pricing of Initial Public Offerings', *Journal of Applied Corporate Finance* 7, 66–74.

Ikenberry, D., J. Lakonishok, and T. Vermaelen, 1995, 'Market Underreaction to Open Market Share Repurchases', *Journal of Financial Economics* 39, 181–208.

Jacquillat, B. C., 1986, 'French Auctions of Common Stock: Methods and Techniques of New Issues, 1966–86', in *Going Public: An International Overview*, Euromobilaire Occasional Paper 2.

Jain, B. A. and O. Kini, 1994, 'The Post-Issue Operating Performance of IPO Firms', *Journal of Finance* 49, 1699–1726.

James, C., 1992, 'Relationship-Specific Assets and the Pricing of Underwriter Services', *Journal of Finance* 47, 1865–1885.

—— and P. Wier, 1990, 'Borrowing Relationships, Intermediation and the Cost of Issuing Public Securities', *Journal of Financial Economics* 28, 149–171.

Jansen, B. and A. Tourani Rad, 1995, 'IPOs and the Morning After: Underwriter Price Support in the Netherlands', mimeo, University of Limburg.

Jegadeesh, N., M. Weinstein, and I. Welch, 1993, 'An Empirical Investigation of IPO Returns and Subsequent Equity Offerings', *Journal of Financial Economics* 34, 153–175.

Jenkinson, T. J., 1990, 'Initial Public Offerings in the United Kingdom, the United States, and Japan', *Journal of the Japanese and International Economies* 4, 428–449.

—— and C. P. Mayer, 1988, 'The Privatisation Process in France and the UK', *European Economic Review* 32, 482–490.

—— and J. M. Trundle, 1990, 'New Equity Issues in the United Kingdom', *Bank of England Quarterly Bulletin*, May, 243–252.

Jensen, M. and W. Meckling, 1976, 'Theory of the Firm: Managerial Behaviour, Agency Costs and Ownership Structure', *Journal of Financial Economics* 3, 306–360.

—— and K. Murphy, 1990, 'Performance Pay and Top Management Incentives', *Journal of Political Economy* 98, 225–264.

Jog, V. M. and A. K. Srivastava, 1996, 'The Canadian Environment for Initial Public Offerings: Underpricing, Long-Term Performance and the Process of Going Public', mimeo, Carleton University, Ottawa.

Johnson, J. M. and R. E. Miller, 1988, 'Investment Banker Prestige and the Underpricing of Initial Public Offerings', *Financial Management* 17, 19–29.

Kaneko, T. and R. H. Pettway, 1994, 'The Effects of Removing Price Limits and Introducing Auctions upon Short-Term IPO Returns: The Case of Japanese IPOs', Working Paper No. 52794, Financial Research Institute, University of Missouri.

Keloharju, M., 1993*a*, 'Initial IPO Returns and the Characteristics of Post-IPO Financing in Finland', mimeo, Helsinki School of Economics and Business Administration.

—— 1993*b*, 'The Winner's Curse, Legal Liability, and the Long-Run Price Performance of Initial Public Offerings in Finland', *Journal of Financial Economics* 34, 251–277.

—— 1996, 'The Anatomy of Finnish IPO Investors', mimeo, Helsinki School of Economics and Business Administration.

Kim, J. B., I. Krinsky, and J. Lee, 1993, 'Motives for Going Public and Underpricing: New Findings from Korea', *Journal of Business Finance and Accounting* 20, 195–211.

—— —— —— 1995, 'The After-Market Performance of Initial Public Offerings in Korea', *Pacific-Basin Finance Journal* 3, 429–448.

Koh, F. and T. Walter, 1989, 'A Direct Test of Rock's Model of the Pricing of Unseasoned Issues', *Journal of Financial Economics* 23, 251–272.

—— J. Lim and N. Chin, 1992, 'The Signalling Process in Initial Public Offerings', *Asia Pacific Journal of Management* 9, 151–165.

Kothari, S. P. and J. B. Warner, 1995, 'Measuring Long-Horizon Security Price Performance', Working Paper No. FR 95-19, University of Rochester.

Kunz, R. M. and R. Aggarwal, 1994, 'Why Initial Public Offerings Are Underpriced: Evidence from Switzerland', *Journal of Banking and Finance* 18, 705–724.

La Chapelle, C. A. and B. M. Neuberger, 1983, 'Unseasoned New Issue Price Performance on Three Tiers: 1975–1980', *Financial Management* 12, 23–28.

Lee, I., 1994, 'Do Firms Knowingly Sell Overvalued Equity?', mimeo, University of Illinois at Urbana-Champaign.

Lee, P. J., S. L. Taylor and T. S. Walter, 1994, 'Australian IPO Pricing in the Short and Long Run', mimeo, University of Sydney.

Leland, H. and D. Pyle, 1977, 'Informational Asymmetries, Financial Structure, and Financial Intermediation', *Journal of Finance* 32, 371–387.

Leleux, B. F., 1992, 'Information and Fads Components in IPO Pricing: A Survival Analysis', mimeo, INSEAD.

Levis, M., 1990, 'The Winner's Curse Problem, Interest Costs, and the Underpricing of Initial Public Offerings', *Economic Journal* 100, 76–89.

—— 1993a, 'The Long-Run Performance of Initial Public Offerings: The UK Experience 1980–1988', *Financial Management* 22, 28–41.

—— 1993b, 'The First 1000 Days in the Life of an IPO', mimeo, City University Business School, London.

—— forthcoming, 'Seasoned Equity Offerings and the Short and Long-Run Performance of Initial Public Offerings in the UK', *European Financial Management*.

Ljungqvist, A. P., 1995a, 'The Timing, Pricing and Long-Term Performance of Initial Public Offerings', unpublished D.Phil. thesis, Nuffield College, Oxford University.

—— 1995b, 'When Do Firms Go Public? Poisson Evidence from Germany', mimeo, Oxford University School of Management Studies.

—— 1996a, 'Can Firms Outwit the Market? Timing Ability and the Long-Run Performance of IPOs', forthcoming in M. Levis (ed.), *Empirical Issues in Raising Equity Capital*. Amsterdam: North-Holland (1996).

—— 1996b, 'Pricing Initial Public Offerings: Further Evidence from Germany', forthcoming in *European Economic Review*.

—— 1996c, 'IPO Long-Run Under-Performance: Fact or Fiction?', mimeo, Oxford University School of Management Studies.

Logue, D., 1973a, 'On the Pricing of Unseasoned Equity Issues, 1965–69', *Journal of Financial and Quantitative Analysis* 8, 91–103.

—— 1973b, 'Premia on Unseasoned Equity Issues, 1965–69', *Journal of Economics and Business* 25, 133–141.

Loughran, T., 1993, 'NYSE vs. NASDAQ Returns: Market Microstructure or the Poor Performance of Initial Public Offerings?', *Journal of Financial Economics* 33, 241–260.

—— and J. R. Ritter, 1994, 'The Operating Performance of Firms Conducting Seasoned Equity Offerings', mimeo, University of Illinois at Urbana-Champaign.

—— —— 1995, 'The New Issues Puzzle', *Journal of Finance* 50, 23–51.

—— —— and K. Rydqvist, 1994, 'Initial Public Offerings: International Insights', *Pacific Basin Finance Journal* 2, 165–199.

Macey, J. and H. Kanda, 1990, 'The Stock Exchange as a Firm: The Emergence of Close Substitutes for the New York and Tokyo Stock Exchanges', *Cornell Law Review* 75, 1007–1052.

Manigart, S. and B. Rogiers, 1992, 'Empirical Examination of the Underpricing of Initial Public Offerings on the Brussels Stock Exchange', mimeo, Vlerick School for Management, University of Ghent.

McGuinness, P., 1992, 'An Examination of the Underpricing of Initial Public Offerings in Hong Kong: 1980–90', *Journal of Business Finance and Accounting* 19, 165–186.

—— 1993a, 'Investor- and Issuer-Related Perspectives of IPO Underpricing', *Omega International Journal of Management Sciences* 21, 377–392.

—— 1993b, 'The Post-Listing Return Performance of Unseasoned Issues of Common Stock in Hong Kong', *Journal of Business Finance and Accounting* 20, 167–194.

Megginson, W. L. and K. A. Weiss, 1991, 'Venture Capitalist Certification in Initial Public Offerings', *Journal of Finance* 46, 879–903.

Michaely, R. and W. H. Shaw, 1992, 'Asymmetric Information, Adverse Selection, and the Pricing of Initial Public Offerings', mimeo, Cornell University.

—— —— 1994, 'The Pricing of Initial Public Offerings: Tests of Adverse-Selection and Signaling Theories', *Review of Financial Studies* 7, 279–319.

Mikkelson, W. H. and K. Shah, 1994, 'Performance of Companies around Initial Public Offerings', mimeo, University of Oregon.

Miller, E. M., 1977, 'Risk, Uncertainty, and Divergence of Opinion', *Journal of Finance* 32, 1151–1168.

Miller, R. E. and F. K. Reilly, 1987, 'An Examination of Mispricing, Returns, and Uncertainty for Initial Public Offerings', *Financial Management* 16, 33–38.

Modigliani, F. and M. H. Miller, 1958, 'The Cost of Capital, Corporation Finance and the Theory of Investment', *American Economic Review* 48, 261–297.

Morck, R., A. Shleifer, and R. W. Vishny, 1988, 'Managerial Ownership and Market Valuation: An Empirical Analysis', *Journal of Financial Economics* 20, 293–315.

Muscarella, C. J. and M. R. Vetsuypens, 1989a, 'A Simple Test of Baron's Model of IPO Underpricing', *Journal of Financial Economics* 24, 125–135.

—— —— 1989b, 'The Underpricing of "Second" Initial Public Offerings', *Journal of Financial Research* 12, 183–192.

Myers, S. C. and N. S. Majluf, 1984, 'Corporate Financing and Investment

Decisions When Firms Have Information that Investors Do Not Have', *Journal of Financial Economics* 13, 187–221.

Pagano, M., F. Panetta, and L. Zingales, 1995, 'Why Do Companies Go Public? An Empirical Analysis', CEPR Discussion Paper No. 1332.

Panagos, V. and G. Papachristou, 1993, 'A Note on the Effectiveness of the Price Guarantee Clause in the Greek Underwriting Contract: Evidence from the After-Market Volatility of IPOs', mimeo, Aristotle University of Thessaloniki, Greece.

Rajan, R. and H. Servaes, 1994, 'The Effect of Market Conditions on Initial Public Offerings', mimeo, University of Chicago.

Reilly, F. K., 1977, 'New Issues Revisited', *Financial Management* 6, 28–42.

Ritter, J. R., 1984, 'The Hot Issue Market of 1980', *Journal of Business* 57, 215–240.

—— 1987, 'The Costs of Going Public', *Journal of Financial Economics* 19, 269–282.

—— 1991, 'The Long-Run Performance of Initial Public Offerings', *Journal of Finance* 46, 3–27.

Rock, K., 1986, 'Why New Issues Are Underpriced', *Journal of Financial Economics* 15, 187–212.

Ruud, J. S., 1990, 'Underpricing of Initial Public Offerings: Goodwill, Price Shaving or Price Support', unpublished Ph.D. dissertation, Harvard University.

—— 1991, 'Another View of the Underpricing of Initial Public Offerings', *Federal Reserve Bank of New York Quarterly Review* 16, 83–85.

—— 1993, 'Underwriter Price Support and the IPO Underpricing Puzzle', *Journal of Financial Economics* 34, 135–151.

Rydqvist, K., 1993, 'Initial Public Offerings in Sweden', Working Paper No. 48, Stockholm School of Economics.

—— 1994, 'Compensation, Participation Restrictions and the Underpricing of Initial Public Offerings', mimeo, Stockholm School of Economics and Carnegie-Mellon University, Pittsburgh.

Safieddine, A. and W. J. Wilhelm, 1996, 'An Empirical Investigation of Short-Selling Activity Prior to Seasoned Equity Offerings', *Journal of Finance* 51, 729–749.

Schultz, P. H. and M. A. Zaman, 1994, 'After-Market Support and Underpricing of Initial Public Offerings', *Journal of Financial Economics* 35, 199–219.

SEC (Securities and Exchange Commission), 1971, *Institutional Investor Study Report of the Securities and Exchange Commission*. Washington, DC: US Government Printing Office.

Shaw, D. C., 1971, 'The Performance of Primary Common Stock Offerings: A Canadian Comparison', *Journal of Finance* 26, 1101–1113.

Shleifer, A. and R. Vishny, 1986, 'Large Stakeholders and Corporate Control', *Journal of Political Economy* 94, 461–488.

Simon, C. J., 1989, 'The Effect of the 1933 Securities Act on Investor Information and the Performance of New Issues', *American Economic Review* 79, 295–318.

Slovin, M. B. and J. E. Young, 1990, 'Bank Lending and Initial Public Offerings', *Journal of Banking and Finance* 14, 729–740.

—— M. E. Sushka, and Y. M. Bendeck, 1994, 'Seasoned Common Stock Issuance Following an IPO', *Journal of Banking and Finance* 18, 207–226.

Smith, C. W., 1986, 'Investment Banking and the Capital Acquisition Process', *Journal of Financial Economics* 15, 3–29.

Spence, A. M., 1974, *Market Signalling*. Cambridge, Mass.: Harvard University Press.

Sternberg, T. D., 1989, 'Bilateral Monopoly and the Dynamic Properties of Initial Public Offerings', mimeo, Vanderbilt University, Nashville.

Stigler, G. J., 1964a, 'Public Regulation of the Securities Markets', *Journal of Business* 37, 117–142.

—— 1964b, 'Comment', *Journal of Business* 37, 414–422.

Stoll, H. R. and A. J. Curley, 1970, 'Small Business and the New Issue Market for Equities', *Journal of Financial and Quantitative Analysis* 5, 309–322.

Stoughton, N. M. and J. Zechner, 1995, 'IPO Mechanisms, Monitoring and Ownership Structure', mimeo, University of California, Irvine.

Stulz, R., 1988, 'Managerial Control of Voting Rights: Financing Policies and the Market for Corporate Control', *Journal of Financial Economics* 20, 25–54.

Teoh, S. H., T. J. Wong, and G. R. Rao, 1993, 'An Empirical Analysis of the Incentives for Earnings Management in Initial Public Offerings', mimeo, University of California, Los Angeles.

—— —— —— 1994, 'Earnings Management and the Long-Term Performance of Initial Public Offerings', mimeo, University of California, Los Angeles.

—— I. Welch, and T. J. Wong, 1995, 'Earnings Management and the Post-Issue Underperformance of Seasoned Equity Offerings', Working Paper 95–7, University of Michigan.

Tinic, S. M., 1988, 'Anatomy of Initial Public Offerings of Common Stock', *Journal of Finance* 43, 789–822.

Titman, S. and B. Trueman, 1986, 'Information Quality and the Valuation of New Issues', *Journal of Accounting and Economics* 8, 159–172.

Van Arsdell, P. M., 1958, *Corporate Finance*. New York: Ronald Press.

Vaughan, G. D., P. H. Grinyer, and S. J. Birley, 1977, *From Private to Public*. Cambridge: Woodhead-Faulkner.

'Verordnung über die Feststellung des Börsenpreises von Wertpapieren vom 17 April 1967', in *Beck-Texte: Bankrecht*, 19th edn. Munich: DTV.

Vos, E. A. and J. Cheung, 1992, 'New Zealand IPO Underpricing: The Reputation Factor', *Small Enterprise Research* 1, 13–22.

Wasserfallen, W. and C. Wittleder, 1994, 'Pricing Initial Public Offerings: Evidence from Germany', *European Economic Review* 38, 1505–1517.

Weiss Hanley, K., 1993, 'The Underpricing of Initial Public Offerings and the Partial Adjustment Phenomenon', *Journal of Financial Economics* 34, 231–250.

Weiss Hanley, K., A. A. Kumar, and P. J. Seguin, 1993, 'Price Stabilisation in the Market for New Issues', *Journal of Financial Economics* 34, 177–197.

—— and W. J. Wilhelm, 1995, 'Evidence on the Strategic Allocation of Initial Public Offerings', *Journal of Financial Economics* 37, 239–257.

Welch, I., 1989, 'Seasoned Offerings, Imitation Costs, and the Underpricing of Initial Public Offerings', *Journal of Finance* 44, 421–449.

—— 1996, 'Equity Offerings Following the IPO: Theory and Evidence', *Journal of Corporate Finance* 2, 227–259.

Wessels, R. E., 1989, 'The Market for Initial Public Offerings: An Analysis of the Amsterdam Stock Exchange (1982–87)', in R. M. C. Guimaraes, B. G. Kingsman, and S. J. Taylor (eds.), *A Reappraisal of the Efficiency of Financial Markets*. Berlin, Heidelberg: Springer-Verlag.

Wethyavivorn, K. and Y. Koo-Smith, 1991, 'Initial Public Offerings in Thailand, 1988–89: Price and Return Patterns', in S. G. Rhee and R. P. Chang (eds.), *Pacific-Basin Capital Markets Research*, vol. 2. Amsterdam: North-Holland.

Wimmers, S., 1988, 'Aktien- und börsenrechtliche Deregulierung: Die Bewertung aktueller Reformvorschläge durch die Börsenneulinge der Jahre 1977–1986', in H. Albach (ed.), *Die private Aktiengesellschaft: Materialien zur Deregulierung des Aktienrechts*. Stuttgart: Poeschel.

Zingales, L., 1995, 'Insider Ownership and the Decision to Go Public', *Review of Economic Studies* 62, 425–448.

INDEX

....

Note: italic page numbers denote references to tables and figures.